British Library Cataloguing in Publication Data

Osband, Gillian
    What Can I Do Indoors?
    1. Indoor games—Juvenile literature
    I. Title   II. Spargo, Bobbie
    793   GV1229

ISBN 0 340 32997 1

Published by Hodder and Stoughton Children's Books,
a division of Hodder and Stoughton Ltd, Mill Road,
Dunton Green, Sevenoaks, Kent TN13 2YJ

Printed in Belgium by Henri Proost & Cie, Turnhout

WHAT CAN I DO INDOORS?

Gillian Osband
Illustrated by Bobbie Spargo

WHAT CAN I DO INDOORS? contains hundreds of things to make and do. Some of them are easy to do. Some require a little thought and practice. Some will start you off on a new hobby. Read the instructions carefully.
Get all the ingredients you need together — and then begin.

Where you need an adult's help — ASK FOR IT! The safety rules in the kitchen and workshop are to stop accidents. Read them carefully!

Now have lots of fun . . . .

HODDER AND STOUGHTON
LONDON SYDNEY AUCKLAND TORONTO

CONTENTS

CONTENTS

GAMES, GAMES, GAMES

PINBALL WIZARD

You Need: Stiff card at least 65cm x 80cm; ruler; pencil; scissors; felt-tip pens; a clean, empty plastic bottle; marbles; sticky tape.

What You Do:

If you follow the instructions carefully, you should have no difficulty making your own **PINBALL MACHINE.** If you do get stuck—ask an adult to help you.

1. MAKE THE BASE

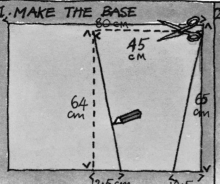

Draw a rectangle 45cm x 64cm on the card. Cut it out. At one end, measure 12.5cm in from each side. Draw lines to the corners as shown. Cut along these lines to make the base.

2.

Mark 10 places for holes. Make them with the end of your scissors. Make the holes slightly smaller than the marbles.

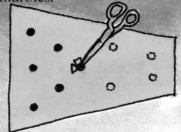

Tip: it may be easier to make the holes if you place the card over an empty jar.

3. MAKE THE SIDES

Cut a piece of card 65cm x 10cm. From both long sides measure 4cm in. Draw lines across. Draw a diagonal line (A-B). Cut along it. Measure 5cm in from the wide end. Cut a slit up to the line. 15cm along, cut another slit up to the line. Fold up the slits.

4 MAKING THE ENDS

Cut a piece of card 45cm x 6cm. Cut two 2cm slits, 15cm apart, in the middle. Cut another piece of card 20cm x 4cm. Fold up the slits.

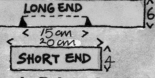

Make the Rebounds:

Draw lines around the bottle, about 3cm apart. Cut up the side of the bottle, then cut along the lines to make strips. Tape them on the sides as shown.

5.

Tape the flaps from the sides and ends to the underneath of the base. Tape the sides and pieces together at the corners.

Paint the base. Number the holes.

HOW TO PLAY:

Use the rebound at the bottom as a spring. Pull it back, put a marble in the middle; let go! Every time it lands in a hole, note the score. Try and keep the marble in play by flipping it off the spring. If it lands either side of the spring, you are out!

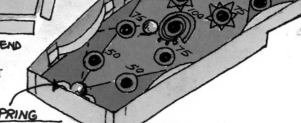

SPRING

MAD MARBLES

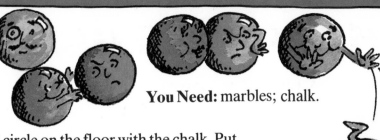

BULL'S EYE
(1 or more players)

You Need: marbles; chalk.

Draw a medium-sized circle on the floor with the chalk. Put 5 marbles in the middle.

The Aim: to clear the circle of marbles.

What You Do: Stand at the edge of the circle and drop a marble from waist height, onto the marbles in the middle. Try and hit a marble to make it roll out of the circle. If the dropped marble stays in the circle, leave it there. If none of the marbles roll out, add one as penalty. How many drops will it take you to clear the circle?

ROLL 'EM!
(1 or more players)

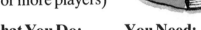

BOOK   TRAY   MARBLES   EMPTY TISSUE BOX

What You Do: **You Need:**

Cut 5 small arches along one side of the box (large enough for the marbles to go through). Write these numbers over the arches— **5, 3, 1, 3, 5.** Put the box at one end of the tray. Put the book under the other end to raise it.

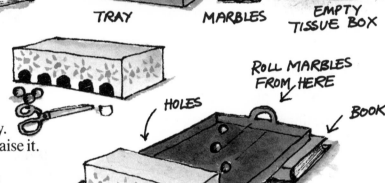

ROLL MARBLES FROM HERE

HOLES

BOOK

How to Play: Roll your marbles, one at a time, and see what score you can get. Take it in turns to roll the 6 marbles. The first to score 30 wins. If you are playing on your own—see how quickly you can do it.

PICK-A-MATCH (1 or more players)

You Need: 30 used matches; poster paints; a mug; tweezers.

What You Do: Brush off the burnt ends from the matches, then dip them in the paint. Dip 5 green; 3 blue; 1 white; 10 yellow; the rest red. Give each colour a score.

How To Play: Put the matches in the mug. Drop them on a flat surface. Pick them up, one at a time. Do not let any of the other matches move, or you are out. Add up your score.

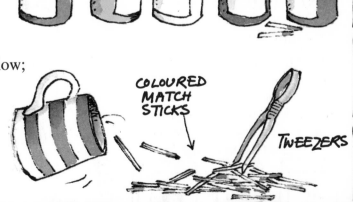

COLOURED MATCH STICKS

TWEEZERS

GAMES, GAMES, GAMES

CRAZY RACES

Ask first! Make sure you don't break anything!

Here are some fiendish ideas for **CRAZY RACES** round the house. Make up your own courses. Time each racer.

1. Start: bottom of the stairs; up to the bathroom; brush your teeth twice; down to the kitchen; drink a glass of water in one go; into the dining room; 7 times round the table; hop back to the start.

2. Work out a route. Each racer has to go round it walking **backwards.** If you bump into anything, start again.

3. Start: front door; crawl to the kitchen; eat a biscuit; up the stairs; bounce 4 times on your bed; down the stairs on your bottom; back to the front door.

TIN TOSS

You Need: 6 empty tins; a ball.

Stand the tins in a pyramid. Stand about 2 metres away (the doorway can be your line). You have 3 throws to knock the whole pyramid over.

BALL BOUNCING

You Need: Empty, numbered food tubs; a ping-pong ball.

Stand the tubs together. Stand about 2 metres away. Try and throw or bounce the ball into a tub. Take it in turns. If it goes in and stays, you win a point. The first to get 10 points wins.

PUFF BALL

You Need: A straw for each player; a ping-pong ball; chalk; card; crayons; empty cardboard box (a shoe box); plasticine.

What You Do: Draw 2 goalkeepers. Cut them out; colour them in; wedge them into plasticine balls. Cut the box in half. With the chalk draw the pitch on the floor or table top. Put the goals (box halves) at each end. Put your goalkeepers in position. Divide into 2 teams. Put the ball in the middle of the line. Blow the ball with your straw. If it blows off the pitch, put it back on the line. Move your goalkeeper, and blow, to stop the ball.

The first team to score 10 wins.

POCKET PUZZLE

You Need: card; pencil; glue; ruler; pens; 5 beads or dried beans.

What You Do:

1. Draw an 8cm square on the card. Cut it out. Draw an inner square 1cm from the sides. Cut as shown. Fold up the sides. Glue the flaps.

Make another box for the lid 1mm larger.

2. With the scissors, make a hole in each corner and in the middle. They must be smaller than the beads or beans.

3. Paint patterns on the base.

How To Play: Put the beans or beads in the box. Try and get them all in the holes. Time yourself. Try and beat your record. Put the lid on when you are not playing.

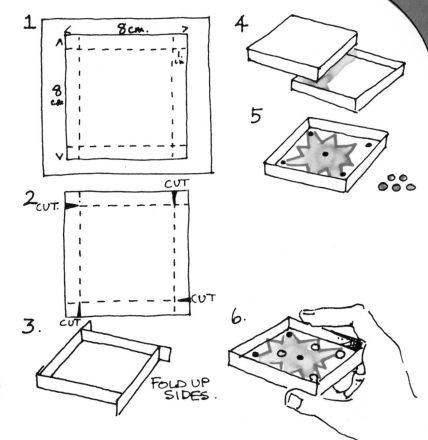

TIPS FOR MAKING YOUR OWN BOARD GAME

You need a piece of card about 30cm square. Mark off every 2cm along each side. Draw lines down and across to make the squares. Number the squares.

For a spy game, draw obstacles on different numbers on the board. If the instructions are simple, for example, **miss 2 turns,** write them on the board.

Colour the board and the pictures on it. Colour some squares bright red. If you land on one of these, you pick up one card from a pile you have made with instructions on them. You may have to crack a code, deliver a secret message or change your appearance, before you can move on.

Make up your own rules. Tell the players!

Draw spies on thin card. Colour them; cut them out and wedge them into plasticine balls for your markers.

Mark dots on a sugar lump for your dice.

You can make any game you can think of . . . space games; Viking invaders; detective . . .

ROBBERS   POLICE

KITCHEN CAPERS!

The great thing about cooking is that you end up with something delicious to eat!

KITCHEN RULES

Always wash your hands before you start.
Wear an apron.
Read the recipe right through.
Get out all the tools and all the ingredients before you begin.
If you have to use sharp knives, **ask an adult** to help.
Ask an adult to light the oven or grill.
Turn everything off when you finish.
Keep saucepan handles **turned away from you.**
Wear oven gloves to hold hot dishes and pans.
Always **mop up** anything spilt at once.
Make sure you don't forget the **time.**
If you burn or cut yourself, put it under cold water and **call an adult at once.**

FACT

You can make a dozen omelettes from one ostrich egg.

Here are a few tasty things you can make to eat....

SCRAMBLED EGGS (For 1)

You Need: 2 eggs; salt; pepper; a little butter; bowl; fork; pan; wooden spoon.

What You Do:

1. Break the 2 eggs into a bowl. Add a pinch of salt and a shake of pepper. Beat the mixture with a fork.

2. Ask for one cooking ring to be turned on or lit at a low level. Put a saucepan or frying pan on the ring. Put in a little butter and let it melt.

3. Add the egg mixture. Cook it slowly over the low heat, stirring it all the time with a wooden spoon, until it begins to go firm and set.

4. When the scrambled egg is beginning to set, take the pan off the ring —and serve. Scrambled eggs are nice to eat with hot buttered toast.

For more than one: you need 2 eggs per person.

CRAZY SANDWICH (Good for birthdays or a special tea)

You Need: A long French loaf; lots of fillings like: cheese, boiled eggs, jam, crisps, sardines, tomatoes.

What You Do:

1. Cut the loaf in half **lengthwise.** Butter the bottom half.

2. Add the fillings in any mix you fancy. You can have the same filling all the way along—or— 3-4 different ones as you go down the loaf.

3. Put the top on and press gently. If it's your birthday, poke holes in the crust and put in candles. Slice up your crazy sandwich!

CORNED BEEF COOK UP (For 6 hungry people)

You Need: 1kg of potatoes; water; salt; 340g tin of corned beef; 1 medium onion; 50g butter or margarine; 450g tin baked beans; pepper; saucepan; frying pan; knife; casserole; sieve; chopping board.

What You Do:

1. Heat the oven to 190°C (375°F) Gas Mark 5.

2. Peel the potatoes. Cut in quarters. Put in a saucepan. Cover with water. Add a pinch of salt. Bring to the boil and cook for 20 minutes. Drain the potatoes in the sieve, rinse in cold water and cut into 3cm cubes.

3. Open the tin of beef. Cut it into 3cm cubes on the board. Peel the onion. Cut it lengthways, then slice it across and lengthways to chop.

4. Melt butter or margarine in frying pan. Add potatoes. Stir over a medium heat until lightly browned. Put a ¼ of them on a plate.

5. Add the onion to the pan. Cook for 5 minutes. Stir a few times. Add the beans, beef and a pinch of salt and pepper. Stir the mixture and cook a few minutes.

6. Put the mixture in the casserole. Put the rest of the potato on top. Bake uncovered, for 20 minutes.

BAKED POTATO

You Need: 1 medium potato per person; a little butter; silver foil; knife.

What You Do:

1. Heat the oven to 190°C (375°F) Gas Mark 5.

2. Make a small slice in the top of each potato. Rub the skin with a little butter.

3. Wrap each potato in silver foil. Bake in the oven for 1 hour. To make sure it is cooked, press it when you take it out. If it is soft, the potato is cooked. **WEAR OVEN GLOVES!**

4. Eat your potato with salt and pepper; or some butter; or sour cream; or grated cheese—or anything you fancy!

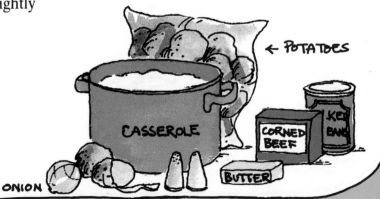

POTATOES

CASSEROLE

CORNED BEEF

KED BANS

BUTTER

ONION

KITCHEN CAPERS!

BAKED BANANAS

You Need: 1 banana per person; butter; sugar; ice-cream; baking dish.

What You Do:

1. Heat the oven to 200°C (400°F) Gas Mark 6.

2. Peel the bananas. Put them in a baking dish. Spread a little butter over them, and then sprinkle them with sugar.

3. Bake them in the oven for 20 minutes. Serve them with ice-cream.

Q. WHAT WOULD YOU CALL TWO BANANAS?

A. A PAIR OF SLIPPERS

FACTS

In 1976 Kathy Wafler took 11 hours 30 minutes to peel an apple weighing 20oz. The peel was 172 feet long when she had finished.

Honey is the only food that lasts and does not spoil. Archaeologists found honey in the tombs of ancient Egyptian pharaohs. The honey was over 2000 years old — and it was still edible.

CRISPY CHOCOLATE CAKE

You Need: A bar of chocolate (milk or plain); corn flakes or rice crispies; saucepan; bowl; plate; spoon.

What You Do:

1. Break the chocolate into pieces. Put in a mixing bowl.

2. Half fill a saucepan with water. Heat it until almost boiling. Turn off the heat. Place the bowl on top of the pan. Wait until the heat of the water melts the chocolate.

3. Stir in 6 tablespoons of corn flakes or rice crispies.

① ② ③ ④

Cover them with chocolate, then put one spoonful at a time on a plate.

They will be ready to eat in 15 minutes.

ORANGE CREAMS

You Need: 400g icing sugar; 1 orange;
½ teaspoon of lemon juice; bowl; grater;
wooden spoon; board; rolling pin;
greaseproof paper.

What You Do:

1. Put the icing sugar in a large bowl.
Press out any lumps with a wooden spoon.

2. Grate the orange rind on to the sugar.
Add the lemon juice and a little orange juice.

3. With clean hands work the ingredients
together to form a smooth paste. If it won't
stay together add a little more orange juice
until it does.

4. Put it on a board. Roll it out until it is
about 1cm thick. If the mixture gets sticky,
rub a little icing sugar on the rolling pin.

5. Cut into squares. Put on some greaseproof paper. Leave them to dry for 2 hours.
Then eat them!

CHOCOLATE PEPPERMINT FIZZ
(For 4 thirsty people)

You Need: 75g plain chocolate;
2 tablespoons sugar; 750 ml milk;
1 teaspoon peppermint essence;
8 tablespoons ice-cream; grater;
saucepan; wooden spoon; jug.

What You Do:

1. Grate the chocolate into the pan.
Add the sugar and 150ml of milk. Heat
gently, stirring all the time, until the sugar
and chocolate melt. Remove from heat.

2. Add the rest of the milk and the
peppermint essence. Stir and pour into a
jug.

3. Chill in the fridge for an hour.
Pour into glasses and add ice cream.

WHICH ONE IS IT?

You Need: 3 eggs. Hard-boil one.

The Trick: Ask your victim which
is the hard-boiled egg and which
are the raw ones. You will tell her
whether she is right or wrong —
and then find the right one.

The Magic: Spin all 3 eggs. The
one that spins easily (the other 2
will wobble) is the hard-boiled one.
Crack it open on your victim's head!

SUPER SPY!

If spying is your business you need to know many different secrets to make you a successful spy—and maybe even the Master Spy!

CARRYING MESSAGES

Secret messages you are carrying **MUST NOT BE FOUND.** You have to **hide** them:

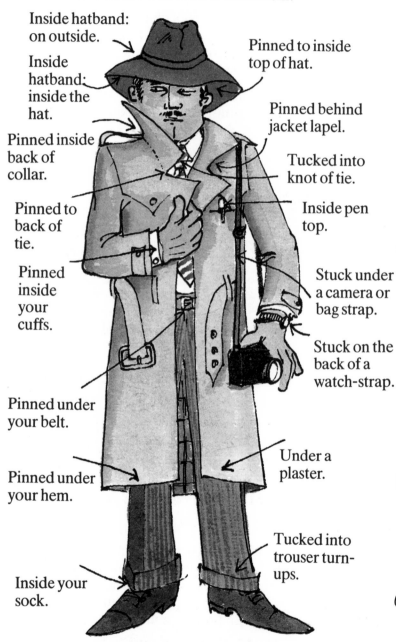

Inside hatband: on outside.

Inside hatband: inside the hat.

Pinned inside back of collar.

Pinned to back of tie.

Pinned inside your cuffs.

Pinned under your belt.

Pinned under your hem.

Inside your sock.

Pinned to inside top of hat.

Pinned behind jacket lapel.

Tucked into knot of tie.

Inside pen top.

Stuck under a camera or bag strap.

Stuck on the back of a watch-strap.

Under a plaster.

Tucked into trouser turn-ups.

Make A False Sole To Your Shoe: Trace your shoe on to a piece of card; cut it out and put it inside your shoe with the message underneath.

DELIVERING YOUR MESSAGE

Now you must deliver your message **secretly!** You **MAKE A DROP!**

① The message is hidden in the dog's collar. The contact pats the dog's head and removes it.

MESSAGE

② A folded newspaper is left on a bench with the message inside.

③ The message is pinned under a bench in the park.

MESSAGE   MESSAGE

④ Put the message in a plastic bag. Bur it in a known spot. The contact pretends to smell the flowers and dig it up.

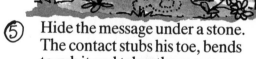

MESSAGE

⑤ Hide the message under a stone. The contact stubs his toe, bends to rub it and takes the message.

MESSAGE

⑥ Hide the message in an empty match box. Drop it. The contact pretends to tie his shoe and picks up the box.

MESSAGE

DISGUISES

You can foil your enemy by disguising yourself.

1. Change your hair by combing it in a different way. Talcum powder will make your hair and eyebrows grey.

2. Put on a hat. Have several hats to confuse your enemy.

3. Put on a pair of glasses with no lenses, or sun glasses.

4. Make a false beard or moustache. Get 2 pieces of string, one to stretch from ear to ear, the other to make room for your mouth. Tie them, as shown. The loops are for your ears. Cut out the shape you want for your beard from cotton wool. For a white beard, just glue it to the string. For a coloured beard, paint it with poster paint, and glue it to the string when dry.

5. Change the colour of your face. Talcum powder makes it paler. Cocoa makes it darker.

6. Put small lumps of cotton wool in your cheeks and between your teeth to change the shape of your face.

7. Black crayon blacks out your teeth.

8. Mix blue and black paint with a little cold cream. Dab it on your face and you look in need of a shave.

9. Use a soft pencil to draw wrinkles.

10. A pebble in your shoe gives you a limp. A ruler tied behind your knee gives you a stiff leg.

TOWEL

CUSHION

RULER

11. A towel across your shoulders or under your jacket, changes your shape. So will cushions tied round your sides or in front.

12. Change your voice. Whisper; talk deep or high or through a smile.

SUPER SPY!

THE MESSAGE

The message must be in code or 'invisible'!

To Make Invisible Ink

Squeeze the juice of an orange, a lemon or a grapefruit into a saucer. With the clean end of a used matchstick, write your message with the juice.

To Read Your Message: hold the paper over a warm radiator or light bulb, and brown writing will appear.

WRITING IN SECRET

To fool your enemy you must write your message in secret code!

SPLITS

The Message: YOUR COVER IS BLOWN

Divide the words in a different way:

YO URCOV ERI SBLO WN

You can also write the words backwards and then divide them in a different way:

NWO LBIS REV OCR VOY

LETTER SWAP

The Message: DO NOT ATTEND THE MEETING TONIGHT

Divide the message into groups of 4 letters

DONO TATT ENDT HEME ETIN GTON IGHT

Then swap the last letter of one word with the first letter of the next one:

DONT OATE TNDH TEME ETIG NTOI NGHT

TYPEWRITER

Choose signs on the typewriter for each letter of the alphabet:

A B C D E F G H I J K L M N O P Q R
° ! " £ $ % & ' ( ) = – # ½ > @ + *
S T U V W X Y Z
? / [: ± ; , <

You can also make up your own signs.

WHICH NUMBER

Each letter of the alphabet is matched with a number. You can start off at any number — which makes deciphering this code very tricky!

For example:

A B C D E F G H I J K L M
31 32 33 34 35 36 37 38 39 40 41 42 43

N O P Q R S T U V W X Y Z
44 45 46 47 48 49 50 51 52 53 54 55 56

Can you decipher this message?

3745 39445045 383934394437

What do you call a spy in bed?

An undercover agent!

What do you call a spy with good manners?

A-gent

14

BODY SIGNALS

Body signals are for emergencies! You can see your contact; you cannot talk to him — but you need to give him an urgent message!

Here are some signals. Invent your own for you and your contact.

SCRATCHING YOUR HEAD

Your cover is blown

COUGHING THREE TIMES

Leave at once.

ARMS FOLDED

Meet me in an hour.

SCRATCHING RIGHT EAR

Go to the drop.

FACTS

Alexander the Great left very large helmets for the enemy to find so they would think he had an army of giants.

Reconnaissance satellites can transmit pictures of anywhere in the world from 240km up in space.

The micro-dot means that a whole type-written page can be reduced to the size of a full stop.

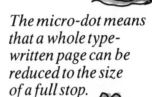

SPY TIPS

*If you think you are being followed look in a shop window. Use the glass as a mirror.

*Always keep in the shade when trailing your quarry or your shadow will give you away.

*Never sign your real name.

*If you have to cross a patch of mud, walk backwards to confuse your enemy.

*A spy must know the area he is working in. Spy out the area first.

*Change your routine every day.

*If you are following bicycle tracks, if you come across 2 tracks, the most recent is the one that cuts across the other.

*Draw a thin pencil line around the papers on your desk. You can then tell if anyone has moved them.

*Try and keep to a hard surface so you don't leave tracks.

*If you hug a suspect when you meet you can tell if they are padded — or if they carry a gun!

*If you think your code and drop have been discovered, leave a false message in your drop giving a new false place to pick up messages. Leave another message in the new drop. If it is collected you know your secret is blown.

PAPER PLAY

PAPER AND PENCIL GAMES

FAMOUS FACES (2 or more players)

Choose a letter of the alphabet, and in 60 seconds write down the names of as many famous people whose surname begins with the chosen letter as you can.

For example: if the letter is '**B**':

Beethoven (composer)
Brigitte Bardot (film star)
Gordon Banks (footballer)

HEAD TO FEET
(Any number)

Choose 2 short words, with the same number of letters, and change one word into the other.

At each stage you must change only **one** letter at a time, and at each step, you must make a real word.

Whoever takes fewest steps is the winner.

For example:
HEAD ... to FEET
HEED
FEED
FEET

Try these steps: **FLOUR** to **BREAD; CAT** to **DOG; WINTER** to **SUMMER.**

ANAGRAMS (any number)

If you re-arrange the letters in a word to make a new word — that is an **ANAGRAM!**

For example: **PRIEST** can become **STRIPE; RIPEST.**

Here are some words for you to find the anagrams:—**ASLEEP; CHESTY; DISEASE; BATTLE; FOREST; GROAN.**

Try to find anagrams with other words too. Who can make the most words?

FACT
An anagram of FUNERAL is REAL FUN.

MIX AND MATCH

You Need: 60 pieces of card, post-card size; scissors; felt-tip pens.

What You Do:

Draw funny noses on 10 cards
Draw funny mouths on 10 cards
Draw funny left ears on 10 cards
Draw funny right ears on 10 cards
Draw funny left eyes on 10 cards
Draw funny right eyes on 10 cards

Keep your 6 piles separate. Shuffle each pile. Then take the top card from each pile — and you'll be amazed at the face you get.

GIANT CUT-OUT

To Make A Poster You Need: a giant piece of paper (a little larger than you); you can glue or sellotape several sheets together, or use a roll of lining paper; pencil; paints; scissors

What You Do:

Lie down on the piece of paper and get a friend to draw round you. Cut yourself out — and paint yourself in. Then stick your giant cut-out on the wall.

To Use Your Cut-Out To Decorate You Will Also Need; water-based fabric dyes; a sheet or large piece of cotton; cartons; paint brush; pins.

To Make The Stencil: Cut round your outline. Pin it on to the sheet or piece of material. Mix up your dyes in the cartons. Paint a line around the cut-out, on to the material. Remove the stencil. Paint yourself in.

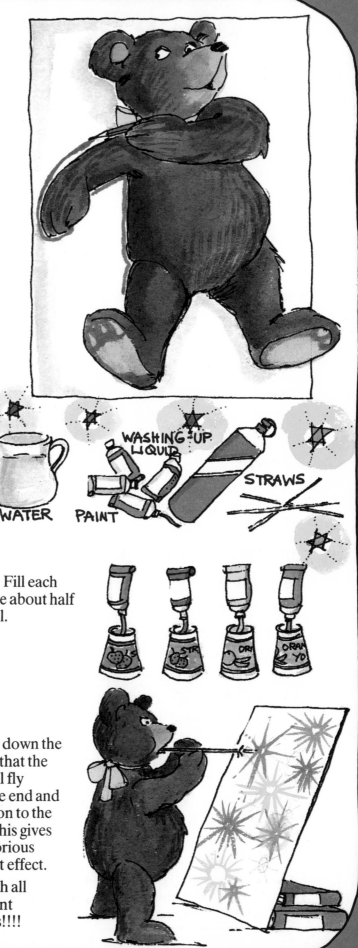

STARBURSTS

You Need:  4 YOGHURT CARTONS

WATER PAINT

WASHING-UP LIQUID

STRAWS

What You Do:

1. Mix the washing-up liquid, water and a different colour paint in each of the yoghurt pots.

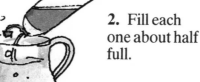

2. Fill each one about half full.

3. Fray the end of the straw by making short tears. Then dip it into one of the pots of paints.

4. Blow down the straw so that the paint will fly out of the end and splatter on to the paper. This gives you a glorious star burst effect.

Do it with all the 4 paint mixtures!!!!

17

PAPER PLAY

PAPER JEWELLERY

Paper Bangles and Beads:

What You Do:

1. Cut the newspaper into long triangles, about 2.5cm at the base, and about 14cm long.

2. Clean off the burnt end of your matchstick. Soak a newspaper triangle in the paste until it is soggy.

3. Starting at the base, roll the triangle tightly round the matchstick, right to the end. Pull your bead off the matchstick, and let it dry.

4. When your beads are dry, paint them in bright colours and varnish them. Then string them together with the needle and thread.

5. For smaller beads, make the base narrower. For longer beads, make it wider.

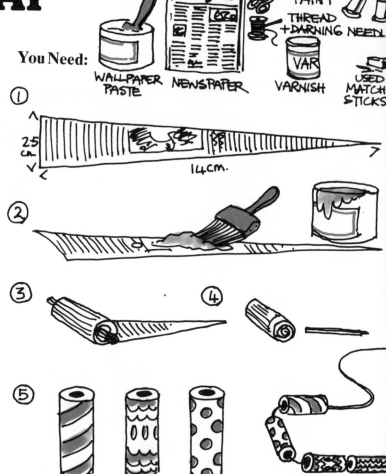

You Need:

WALLPAPER PASTE NEWSPAPER VARNISH USED MATCH STICKS

SCISSORS
PAINT
THREAD
+ DARNING NEEDL

① 2.5 cm — 14cm.
②
③ ④
⑤

PAPER PILOT'S CAP

You Need: A single sheet of newspaper.

What You Do:

1. Fold the sheet in half.

2. Fold the right and left-hand corners (A & B) half-way, as shown.

3. Fold the **front** flap half way, then fold it the rest of the way up.

4. Turn the paper over. Fold the left and right edges (C & D) by the dotted lines shown in the picture.

5. Fold the **back** flap up. First half way, then all the way. Tuck the bottom edge of the flap behind C & D.

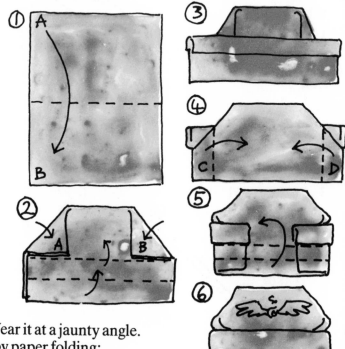

① A B
② A B
③
④ C D
⑤
⑥

Open your pilot's cap out at the bottom. Wear it at a jaunty angle. Here are a few other things you can make by paper folding: a boat; a bird; a box; a cup; a pirate's hat.

FLYING WITCH CARD

You Need:

2 PIECES OF CARD

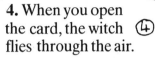

PAINTS GLUE SCISSORS STRING

What You Do:

1. Fold the larger piece of card in half. Paint the witch's house on it.

2. Make a small hole in the top right corner with the point of your scissors. The hole needs to go through both halves of the card. Push the string through both holes. Knot it at the back of the card.

① FOLD

②

③

3. Draw your witch on the smaller piece of card. Paint her and cut her out. Put the witch on the card 'on the ground'. The string needs to go under the broomstick. You may need to cut it. Glue the broomstick to the string.

4. When you open the card, the witch flies through the air.

You can also make a cat climb a tree; a bird fly or a space-ship take off.

TREASURE CHEST

You Need:

CARD 8 EMPTY MATCH BOXES GLUE SPRAY PAINT BEADS COTTON WOOL

What You Do:

1. Push out the matchbox middles. Glue the boxes together, as shown.

2. Lay it on its back on the card and draw round it. Cut it out and glue on to the back of your chest.

3. Put the 'drawers' back. Spray the chest. Glue beads or beans on the front of each drawer as knobs.

4. Glue beans and beads over your chest to decorate. Paint them different colours.

5. Line the drawers with cotton wool for your treasures.

JIGSAWS (2 or more players)

You Need: Paper and pencil for each player.

How To Play: Each player draws a picture. The more detailed, the better (have a set time). Then each player tears his picture into an agreed number of pieces, say 35, and passes the pieces to the player on his left. The first person to put the pieces into their original position to make the picture — wins.

FACTS

The pulp from one tree makes enough paper for only 3000 newspapers.

The letter most used in the English language is 'E'. 'Q' is the least used letter.

The typing exercise: 'The quick brown fox jumps over the lazy dog,' contains all the letters of the alphabet.

FOOL YOUR FRIENDS!

IT'S IMPOSSIBLE!

What You Do: Get your victim or victims to stand with their right shoulder and right foot touching the wall. Then ask them to lift their left leg **without** moving their right foot or shoulder.

I TOLD YOU I COULD DO IT.!!

IT'S IMPOSSIBLE TO DO!!!

You **cannot** balance without moving away from the wall!

THE IMPOSSIBLE JUMP!

What You Do: Tell your victim that you can put your magic coin somewhere where they will not be able to jump over it. Your victim will tell you that's impossible!

Put the coin **ON TOP OF THEIR HEAD!!!**

THE UNBREAKABLE MATCHSTICK

What You Do: Tell your victim that only a superman can break your magic matchstick. Your victim will laugh! Ask for their hand and place the matchstick between their fingers, like this:

Ask them to break it without bending their fingers. **IT'S UNBREAKABLE!!!**

Here are some wicked tricks for you to play!

TRICKY TRICKS

TRICK SUGAR LUMPS

You Need: a piece of white sponge about 1cm thick.

What You Do: Cut squares out of the sponge so that they are the same size as the sugar lumps you use. Mix them in with the real sugar lumps. When your victim puts sugar in their tea or coffee — their sugar will float!

SPONGE

SMUDGY NOSE

You Need: some lipstick or eye shadow.

What You Do: Put a little eye shadow or lipstick on your first finger and forefinger. Find your victim! Tell them to stand still while you wipe a smudge off their nose. **YOU GIVE THEM A SMUDGY NOSE!**

FALSE FANGS   **You Need:** orange pee

What You Do: Cut the orange into quarters. Peel off the fruit from one quarter and cut teeth with a knife, as shown. Wedge one half under your top lip, and the other half under your bottom lip. Act normally until the chosen moment!

CUT

GRRRRR

FLOWER WATER PISTOL

You Need: an empty plastic tube with a screw top; a plastic straw; a coloured plastic bag; a paper-clip; water-proof glue; thin thread; scissors.

What You Do:

1. Take off the cap. Make a small hole in the middle with the scissors. Push the straw into the hole. Put glue round the join.

2. Straighten the paperclip. Then bend it and put 3/4 of it down the straw.

3. Cut 4 squares from the plastic bag. Put them on top of each other and cut out a flower. Make a small hole in the middle.

4. Put the straw through the hole. Tie the base of the flower to the straw with the thread.

5. Fill the tube with water. Put the straw through your button-hole and pull it through. Screw the cap on the tube — then look for your victim to smell your flower!!

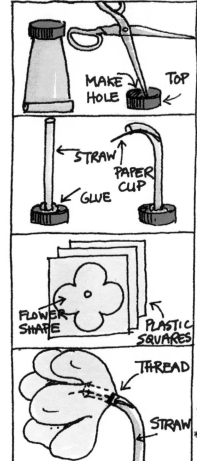

MAKE HOLE — TOP

STRAW — PAPER CLIP — GLUE

FLOWER SHAPE — PLASTIC SQUARES

THREAD — STRAW

1. APPLE PIE BED

Choose your victim. Then: Take all the sheets and blankets off your victim's bed. Put on the bottom sheet. Tuck in the top half only.

3.

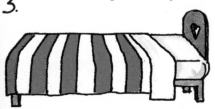

Put the blankets back on. Fold the top of the sheet back over the top of the blankets and tuck in the sides.

2.

Fold the bottom, untucked half, back over.

4.

It will now look like the top sheet that is no longer there, and your victim's bed looks no different from usual . . . until he gets in!!!

HOPPING MAD

A really wicked thing to do is to sew up the bottom of your victim's pyjamas!

YOU: If frozen water is iced water, what's frozen ink?

VICTIM: Iced ink.

YOU: You stink! Well, you said it!

NUMBER FUN

QUITE INCREDIBLE!

If you lived for a million seconds, you'd only live for **12 days.**

12345679 is an amazing number. You can multiply it by 9 or any of the first nine multiples of 9, and the answer will be a **repetition** of the same digit. What is even more amazing, is that the digit will be the same as the number of 9's in the multiplier.

12345679	x	9	=	11111111111
12345679	x	18	=	22222222222
12345679	x	27	=	33333333333
12345679	x	36	=	44444444444
12345679	x	45	=	55555555555
12345679	x	54	=	66666666666
12345679	x	63	=	77777777777
12345679	x	72	=	88888888888
12345679	x	81	=	99999999999

1	x	8	+	1	=	9
12	x	8	+	2	=	98
123	x	8	+	3	=	987
1234	x	8	+	4	=	9876
12345	x	8	+	5	=	98765
123456	x	8	+	6	=	987654
1234567	x	8	+	7	=	9876543
12345678	x	8	+	8	=	98765432
123456789	x	9	+	9	=	987654321

There are other extra-ordinary sums you can do. Look in other number books to find them, or try experimenting yourself to see if you can work them out.

10 TERRIBLE TWISTERS

One orange porridge
Two tugs toil Tynewards
Three thrice-freed thieves
Four fat friars frying fat fish
Five frantic frogs fled fifty fierce fish
Six savoury sausages sizzling
I see seven silent seagulls soaring south
Eight elephants ate eagerly
Nine nice nieces nestle nicely in Nice
Twiddle tightly twisted twine ten times

NUMBER JOKES

Traffic Policeman: *When I saw you driving down the street, lady, I thought '60 at least!'*
Lady Driver: *Oh no, officer! It's this hat. It makes me look a lot older.*

Would you like to buy a pocket calculator, sir?

No thanks. I know how many pockets I've got.

Tom: *Mum, how much am I worth to you?*
Mum: *Why, you're worth more than a million to me!*
Tom: *In that case, can you advance me 25p.*

Emma: *I've added these figures 10 times.*
Teacher: *Good girl.*
Emma: *And here are the 10 different answers.*

Teacher: *Now Susie. If I had two hamburgers, and you had two hamburgers, what would we have?*
Susie: *Lunch!*

LUNCH

Handwritten numbers scattered around the page: 7, 350, 332806.5, 1317, 99, 53, 91.6, 1001, 808, -077, 015760, 404, 19, 36, 978, 27, 17632, 3.70, 7, 20, 44, .77707, 15, 102, -2, 8105, .13.57, 8750, 560, 76, 91, 1086, 130, 5765, 353, 18

TALKING CALCULATORS

Your calculator can talk to you — if you know how! It has a small vocabulary because it can only use 8 letters of the alphabet. Press these numbers to get them:

8 gives B
3 gives E
6 or 9 gives G
4 gives H
1 gives I
7 gives L
0 gives O
5 gives S

To see the letters you need to turn your calculator upside down. To spell out a word you need to press the numbers in reverse order.

For example: to get **GIGGLE** press **379919.**
How many words can you make?

PLAY IT ON THE CALCULATOR

Aim: To be the first player to bring the total to 21 exactly. **(2 players)**

What You Do:

Player 1: presses a number from 1–9. Both the players write the number on a piece of paper.
Player 2: presses the + sign, then a number of his choice between 1–9, but NOT the number pressed by Player 1. Write the number down.
Each player then takes it in turns to add a number between 1–9 which has **not been previously used** to try and reach 21 exactly. Play cannot stop until 21 has been passed or reached.

HOW MANY?

Ask yourself a question:
How many toffees in the packet?
How many times can I hop in a minute?
How heavy is my school case?

Guess the answer — and then measure, weigh or count out the number.

THINK OF A NUMBER

Ask your friend to think of a number — and you will know what it is!

What You Do:

Get your friend to think of a number, for example: **7**
Then ask them to multiply it by 3: **21**
Add 2: **23**
Multiply by 3: **69**
Add a number that is 2 more than the number first thought of (in this case 9 as the original number was 7): **78**
Answer: The number of **tens** in the final number will give you the number.
Your friend originally thought: **7.**

NUMBERS, NUMBERS, NUMBERS

Make your own **NUMBERS DICTIONARY.** Every time you come across a word connected with numbers, for example: digit; calculator; numerical — find out what it means, and write down the word and the meaning in your dictionary.

23

DRESSING UP

Who would you like to be today? Get your imagination going — and dress up!

YOUR DRESSING UP BOX

Here are just a few useful things for your dressing up box:
A large box!

Clothes:
- nighties
- pyjamas
- belts
- scarves
- shawls
- old blankets
- old curtains
- slippers
- hats
- old tights
- shirts
- jackets
- boots
- pieces of bright material

Things:
- spray cans of paint
- paper cups
- paper plates
- wire
- paper-clips
- kitchen foil
- cotton wool
- plastic bags
- ping-pong balls
- sun glasses
- umbrella
- plasticine
- old spectacle frames

YOUR MAKE-UP BOX

You need a special box for your make-up. Ask everybody for their old: lipsticks; face powder; rouge; eye shadow; nail polish; cold cream.

You also need: tissues; cotton wool for a powder puff; a sponge for body make-up.

For lightening: talcum powder; flour or icing sugar.

For darkening: coffee (ask first); earth; charcoal.

For colouring: Mix different-coloured eye shadow or powder paints with a little water.

For sticking: sellotape; double-sided tape; Cow gum or wall-paper paste.

> **TIP: Watch how people of different ages and nationalities move.**

HOW TO MAKE A WIG

You Need: A balloon; newspaper; wall-paper paste.

What You Do:

1. Blow up the balloon to about the size of your head.

2. Tear the newspaper into 5cm squares.

3. Stick the squares over the balloon. Do 4 layers but don't cover the area around the neck.

4. Put it in a warm place for a week.

5. Pop the balloon with a pin. Gently pull it away from the paper shell.

6. Carefully trim the shell so it is large enough to cover your hair. Trim a little at a time.

7. Glue on the 'hair'.

For the hair: You can use — wool; paper; crêpe paper; string or fur fabric. If you need to colour it, dip it in paint and let it dry before you glue it on. Make different wigs.

① BLOW UP BALLOON

② PASTE SQUARE OF PAPER OVER BALLOON

③ TRIM SHELL UNTIL LARGE ENOUGH TO FIT HEAD

WOOL HAIR   FUR HAIR   CREPE PAPER

CHANGING YOUR SHAPE

Tying cushions in the right place alters your shape. Sew string or tape to each corner for tying.

For example:
A long thin cushion tied to the top of your chest gives you a barrel chest. Small cushions tied just above the elbows gives you biceps.

CHANGING YOUR APPEARANCE

Here are a few simple ideas:

Lumps:

You Need: Flesh-coloured plasticine; double-sided tape; make up or paints.

What You Do: Knead the plasticine until it is soft. Put the tape on the underside and stick it to your skin. Smooth the edges and blend the join with make-up or paint. You can also use cotton wool, and paint it.

Beards and Moustaches:

You Need: Cardboard or canvas; pencil; glue; scissors; 'hair' (see WIGS).

What You Do: Fold the cardboard or canvas in half. Draw the shape of the beard or moustache you want on it. Make sure the beard is wide enough to go round your chin. Cut it out. Unfold it. Stick on your hair. Stick them on to you with tape.

Bald Head:

You Need: An old bathing hat, or large plastic bag; sellotape; skin-coloured paint; scissors.

What You Do: Paint the cap or bag. When it is dry, tuck your hair inside.
With the cap: camouflage the join with foundation.
With the bag: Cut a circle large enough to cover your head. Make tucks around the edge to fit your head. Tape them together. Camouflage the join.

Eyebrows:

For Large Ones: Draw the shape on a piece of card. Put another piece behind it and cut out your 2 eyebrows. Stick 'hair' on. Stick them on with double-sided tape.

For Small or Thin Ones: Cover up your own with foundation; toothpaste or coffee paste to match your skin. Draw your new eyebrows with a soft pencil or wax crayons.

Noses:

You Need: Flesh-coloured plasticine; double-sided tape ; cotton wool.

What You Do: Build up the shape you want on your nose with the plasticine.
For Dark Skin: Knead into the plasticine coffee-water paste.
MAKE SURE YOU NEVER BLOCK YOUR NOSTRILS.
With False Nostrils: paint the insides black.

For an Extra Large Nose: Tape cotton wool over the bridge and to your cheek bones. Put the plasticine over it.

Teeth:
NEVER PUT GLUE IN YOUR MOUTH!

You Need: Double-sided tape; thin card.

Black Out Teeth: by sticking a piece of black paper over the tooth or teeth.

For Dracula Teeth: Roll a piece of paper into a cone. Tape it together. Cut the end straight. Fix it over your tooth.

For Large Teeth: Stick rectangles of white card over your teeth, cut to the size you want.

DRESSING UP

Wrinkles:

Look at elderly people to see where wrinkles form. Main wrinkles are on the forehead; around the eyes and from nose to mouth.

Use soft brown pencil or wax crayon. Shade away from the line. Practise!

Scars:

Put a line of Cow gum where you want the scar. Then pinch your skin into a fold and wait for the gum to dry.
To Make It Ugly: use lipstick or crayon.

SOFT PENCIL

COW GUM

Colouring Your Body:

Use thinly mixed water colours or powder paints in the colour you want to be. Put it on with a sponge.

Bruises:

Mix blue and black water colours or powder paints. Dab your bruise on with a sponge or cotton wool.

BLACK AND BLUE WATERCOLOUR

Fingernails:

You Need: Tracing paper; thin card; pencil; scissors; double-sided tape.

What You Do: Trace your own finger-nails on to the card. Extend the nails; make some jagged; paint them and cut them out. Stick them over your own. You can do the same with toenails.

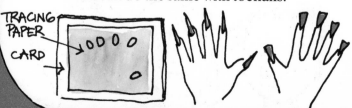

TRACING PAPER

CARD

COSTUME TIPS

Cloaks: curtains; blankets; old pieces of material; dust-bin liner cut open.

Peasant Smock: Cut the collar and cuffs from an old shirt. Belt it, or tie a scarf or strip of material round the middle as a sash.

CUT COLL & CUF

Peasant Trousers: Use pyjama trousers. Tie around the bottom of each leg with string or material. Bunch the trousers over. The baggier the better. Or — cut them off at the knee.

TIE

Waistcoat: Use a bright piece of material. Cut out the shape of the front of a waistcoat. (Try and borrow one and draw round it.) Pin it to your shirt.

SAFETY PINS

From Outer Space: Spray wellingtons and rubber gloves silver or gold (ask first!). Stick on glitter. A black plastic bin liner, cut open and then to size, with foil stuck on one side, makes a cloak.

Helmet: Use a plastic salad bowl or colander. Cover with kitchen foil. Cut nose or ear pieces from card. Paint them silver and tape on.

FOIL

Banner; Spear; Trident: Paint an old broom handle.

Banner: Paint a design on material. Cut it to the shape you want. Sew tape to the top and bottom of one side. Tie it to the top of the broom.

Spear: Cut out a piece of card for the top of the spear. Paint it silver. Glue it to the top of the broom.

Trident: Use 3 squares of foil. Stick one to the top; wrap it round the handle. Make it into a point going straight up. Do the same with the other 2 squares to make points on either side.

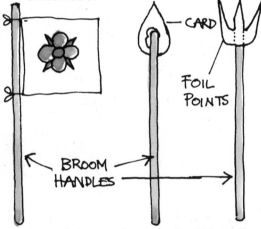

BROOM HANDLES

CARD

FOIL POINTS

Sword: Draw the sword and handle on stiff card. Cut it out. Paint the sword silver and the handle gold.

For a Rapier: Try and use a piece of dowelling. For the handle, cut a soft sponge ball in half. Stick the rod through it. Paint them both.

Shields: Draw the shape you want on card. Cut it out. Draw a design on it and paint it. Or spray it silver.

On the back: Staple a loop of card big enough to put your hand through.

BACK OF SHIELD

½ BATH SPONGE

Making Patterns: see Groovy Clothes and Printing Craft for stencilling material.

Brocade; Embroidery: For a richly embroidered panel for a dress or jacket:- tear up enough tissue paper or dry leaves to cover the panel. Spread the panel with paste and glue on the paper or leaves. When dry, spray in silver or gold and sew it on.

Jewellery: You can make exotic jewellery from card. Paint it silver or gold. Stick on beads, shells etc.

Shoe Buckles: Cut out 2 squares, the same size, in card. Make 2 slits in the middle. Paint them silver. Thread ribbon through the slits and tie under your shoe.

Masks: Paint your 'face' on one side of a paper bag. Cut out holes for your eyes, nose and mouth. You can also make a half mask ending at your nose.

These are just a few ideas. Many accessories can be made from card if you think carefully how to make them.

Remember: when you have decided who you are going to be, try and find costumes of the period, or the character you want to be, to see what they wore. Then use your imagination to turn what you have or can make into your character.

For example: to become a **gangster's moll:** satin-type slip; high-heeled shoes; beads; bangles; sash; bright-red lips; thin eyebrows; hair parted on the side or in a bun.

Borrow books from the library to show you how to make complete outfits.

GROOVY CLOTHES

Here are some simple ideas to brighten up your clothes — and to change something old into something new.

BADGES

Felt is the easiest material to use for badges because the edges do not fray. You can buy small squares of felt in very bright colours.

What You Do:

Draw your shape on the felt with a pencil. Cut it out and sew it on your skirt, jumper, or whatever you like — by over-stitching.

You can use several shapes or patterns to make a picture. You can also use coloured silks to add details to your badges.

Here are some shapes to use. Trace them; cut them out and then pin your trace on to your felt. Either cut straight round them, or draw round them first and then cut them out.

ON JEANS' POCKET

← AROUND SKIRT HEM

EMBROIDER PICTURES

Here are some simple embroidery stitches:

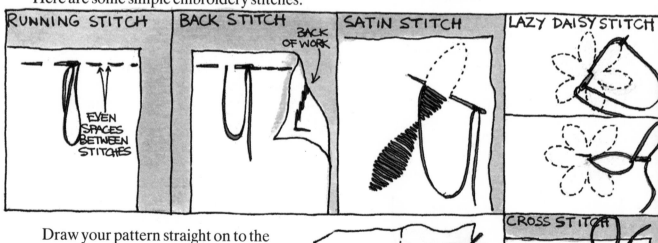

RUNNING STITCH — EVEN SPACES BETWEEN STITCHES

BACK STITCH — BACK OF WORK

SATIN STITCH

LAZY DAISY STITCH

CROSS STITCH

Draw your pattern straight on to the material, or copy a design. To do this, trace the outline on to a small piece of tracing paper. Pin it to the material. Sew through the tracing with small running stitches. Then pull the tracing paper away carefully, and you will have the outline stitches on your material. You can then fill in the pattern and add extra details.

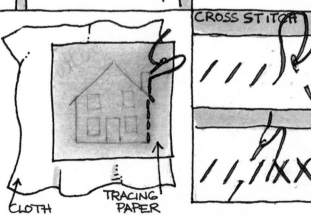

CLOTH   TRACING PAPER

PATCHES

Patches and patchwork patterns add bright splashes of colour to your clothes.

To Make Patchwork Squares:

You Need: Thin card; several different pieces of material; scissors; needle and cotton.

What You Do:

1. Draw out one square on the card. For example, 4cm x 4cm.

2. Cut it out. Use it as the base to cut out several more squares. These are called **templates.**

3. Pin the square to one piece of material. Cut a square out slightly larger than the template. Tack the material round the template, as shown, by folding it over the edge of the card.

4. Do this with as many patches as you want for your pattern. Use different materials.

5. Sew the patches together by holding the edges together and using over-stitch. Try not to sew the card too! Take out the tacking. Pull out the template.

6. Press the patches on the wrong side. Pin them to your jacket, skirt or jeans, and sew them on with over-stitch.

You can do the same with hexagonal shapes. You can also cut out crazy shapes.

① CUT SQUARE TEMPLATE

② DRAW AROUND TEMPLATE ONTO FABRIC.

③ TACK MATERIAL AROUND TEMPLATE.

BACK OF TEMPLATE

④ SEW EDGES NEATLY TOGETHER.

BLOUSE WITH HEXAGONAL PATTERN

SKIRT AND SQUARE PATCHES

TROUSERS WITH CRAZY SHAPES

AN EASY TO MAKE BAG

You Need: A piece of felt about 38cm long and 15cm wide; coloured silks; popper; pins; cord about 1 metre; small piece of felt for the loop.

What You Do:

1. Measure 13.5cm along the edge. Put a pin in as a marker. Measure another 13.5cm along. Mark with a pin.

2. Fold the felt by the first pin and pin both sides at the second pin.

3. With the silk sew along each edge in back stitch or small running stitches.

4. Fold the top flap over. Sew on the popper.

5. Either sew the cord on each side for a shoulder bag — or — sew the loop on the back to put your belt through .

POPPER UNDER HERE.

Decorate your bag with shapes or embroidery.

GROOVY CLOTHES

PRINTING PATTERNS ON YOUR CLOTHES

You Need:

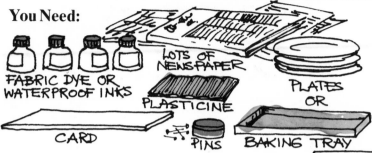

FABRIC DYE OR WATERPROOF INKS

LOTS OF NEWSPAPER

PLATES OR

PLASTICINE

CARD

PINS

BAKING TRAY

* Use fabric dye or waterproof inks.
* Follow the instructions on th dye.
* Put down a lot of newspaper. you do get dye on anything w it off immediately with a clea rag.
* Try your patterns out on scra of material first.
* Print dark colours on light-coloured material.

Ask First!

What You Do:

1. Spread newspaper all round you. Stuff what you are printing on with newspaper so the dye does not go straight through.

2. Put your dye or ink on the trays or plates. Experiment with mixing colours.

3. Make shapes on plasticine printing blocks (p.33) — or cut out patterns on the card and stick them with pins on to plasticine blocks.

4. You can also use stencils of shapes or letters to print words.

5. Cover your printing blocks with paint and use your stencils as shown on p.34.

6. Wait for the paint to dry before removing the newspaper.

STUFF WITH NEWSPAPER

PUT THE DYE OR INK ON THE TRAYS

PINS

PLASTICINE

CUT PATTERNS ON CARD AND PIN TO PLASTICINE

PRINT ON CLOTHES

Customer: *I want to try that dress on in the window.*
Shop Assistant: *I'm sorry madam, you'll have to try it on in the changing room.*

TYE AND DYE

Tye dying can be tricky — so practise first on a piece of scrap material.

You Need: 2-3 fabric dyes; plain material; string or elastic bands; old baking trays.

What You Do:

1. Take a handful of material. Fold it; pleat it or scrunch it up. Tie it tightly with string or an elastic band — pleated, folded and scrunched.

2. Do this in several places round your tee-shirt or skirt.

3. Put your dye on the tray. Put your scrunched up bundle of material in the dye. Do this with each scrunched up bit.

4. Let it dry. Then undo the string. You will get wonderful patterns because the folds will have stopped the dye reaching parts of the material.

5. Fold it in a different way. Re-tie and put each bundle — or some of them — in a different-coloured dye. The patterns will be beautiful because in some places the 2 colours will combine to make a third.

DRY AND REMOVE KNOTS

TIP: Dye in the palest colour first. Wet the tied fabric before putting it in the dye. Wash the material, even if still tied, between one dye and the next.

ODD OLD CLOTHES

Ask members of your family if you can look through their old clothes. Hats, caps, a waistcoat from an old suit, vests, shirts, scarves, belts and jumpers all have tremendous new possibilities for you.

Make sure they don't want them first!

FACT

Silk comes from silk worms fed on mulberry leaves. The Chinese kept this a secret from the rest of the world for 3000 years.

FACTS

Before 1700 boys wore ankle length dresses until the age of 5. Then they wore breeches, loose trousers that came to their knees, and they were then said to be 'breeched'.

George Washington used to soak his ivory dentures in port every night. He thought it would improve their flavour.

In 1885 a 24-year old girl jumped 76m from Clifton Suspension Bridge. She landed unhurt! Her voluminous dress and petticoats acted as a parachute!

PRINTING CRAFT

Printing is easy, messy and fun. Here are a few ideas of how you can print pictures, and some of the things you can make with your prints.

Before you start, cover the surface you are working on with newspaper.

MAKE A PRINTING PAD

Cut a square of thick cotton wool. Put it on a flat plate. Pour poster paint on it. Press your printing blocks or vegetables on the pad to cover them with paint. Try using matchboxes, straws, buttons or toilet roll tubes as printing blocks.

TIP: **Put your printing pad on top of a wad of newspapers to give a firm base for the prints. Poster and powder paints are good for printing.**

BUTTONS

COINS

MATCHBOX

STRAWS

ROLL

HAND PRINTS

You Need: coloured paints; paper; several printing pads.

To make clear prints using your fingers and hand, use **sticky** not runny paint.

Press different parts of your hand on the paint on the pad. See the different shapes you can make with the parts of your hand. Use them to make up pictures.

PAINTS

PAPER

PRINTING PADS

VEGETABLE PRINTS

Vegetables also make good printing blocks. Press them on the pad, then on your paper. See what lovely shapes you can make.

With potatoes, cut them in half. Then cut shapes or holes in the surface with a table knife.

Print patterns or make pictures with the different shapes.

RADISH

CARROT

CAULIFLOWER

To make one tonne of paper you need one tonne of coal.

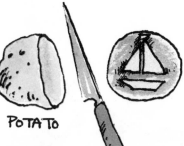

POTATO

SPONGE PRINTS

Draw a design, like a fish or a star, on the sponge with a felt-tip pen. Cut out the shape. Glue your shape on to the piece of wood.

Dip the sponge in the paint — and press it gently on the paper. Add extra details to your print with felt-tip pens.

YOU NEED:

SPONGE

GLUE

SCISSORS

WOOD BLOCK

FELT-TIP PENS

1.

2.

3.

MAKE A DABBER

Stuff a square of cotton with some other pieces of cotton, as shown. Tie them in with a piece of thread round the neck.

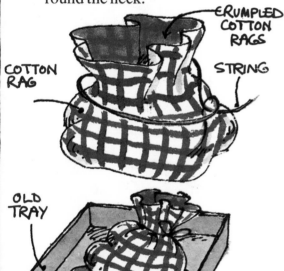

CRUMPLED COTTON RAGS

COTTON RAG

STRING

OLD TRAY

PAINT

FACTS

The first printing press in America was set up by Stephen Day, in Cambridge, Massachusetts, in 1640.

Where letters are printed, they are always put in position back to front, so that when they are printed on paper they appear the right way round.

Some printing machines, called offset machines, which are able to print four colours at great speed, are as large as a house.

PARTY PRINTS

USE WATERPROOF INKS

Trace the shape and size of the paper plates on to a piece of paper. Cut it out. Then cut out patterns to make a stencil. Put it on the plate. With waterproof inks dab the stencil to make pretty patterned plates.

Make strips of roller prints (p.35). Cut them out and glue round the top of the paper cups. Cut out place mats from plain paper. Roller print borders and make patterns in the middle with your printing blocks.

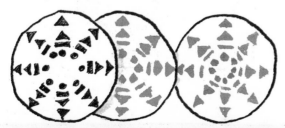

PRINTING CRAFT

STUNNING STENCILS

You Need: PAINTS; BRUSHES; CHALKS; PAPER; INTERESTING OBJECTS; CHAIN; COINS; NUTS; LEAVES; NET; COMB; FEATHER

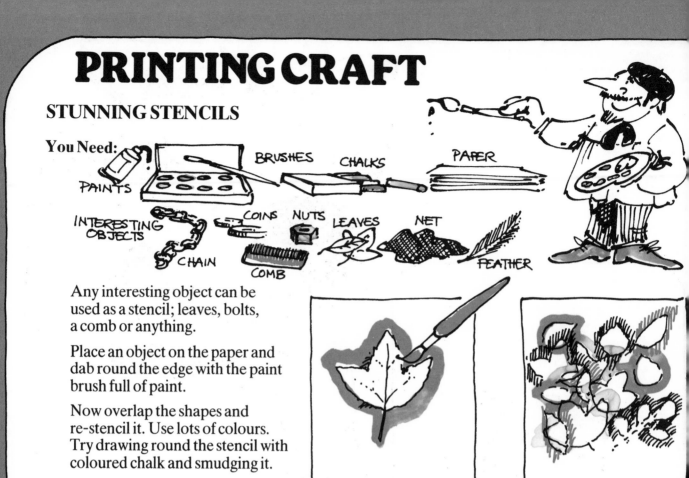

Any interesting object can be used as a stencil; leaves, bolts, a comb or anything.

Place an object on the paper and dab round the edge with the paint brush full of paint.

Now overlap the shapes and re-stencil it. Use lots of colours. Try drawing round the stencil with coloured chalk and smudging it.

STENCIL CARDS... A GHOSTLY SCENE!

You Need: thin card; paper for your cards; poster paint; scissors; pencil; dabber.

If you want a ghostly scene, draw the shapes of trees, bats, a ghost, the moon, on the card. Cut them out. Arrange them on paper. Dip your dabber in the paint (for each colour you need a different dabber). Dab round the edge of your stencils with the paint. When the paint is dry, remove the stencils. You will have an amazing scene! You can do this with **any** shapes.

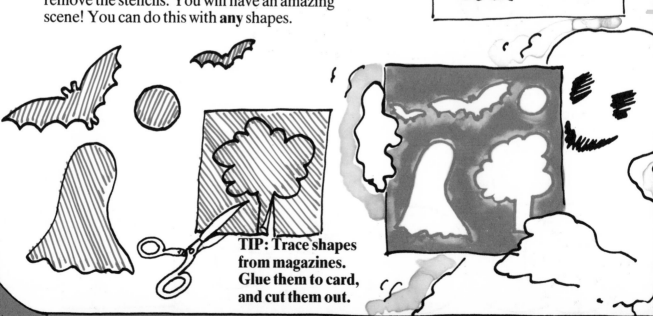

TIP: Trace shapes from magazines. Glue them to card, and cut them out.

ROLLER PRINTS

Cotton reel

2 pencils

Poster paints

Plasticine

Paper

Baking tray

You Need:

What You Do:

1. Cover the cotton reel with a thin layer of plasticine. Push one of the pencils through the holes. (You may need to use a knitting needle instead)

2. With the other pencil, press shapes into the plasticine. Press hard to make them clear.

3. Roll the cotton reel in the paint on the baking tray. Roll it across the paper. When you change paints, wash the roller well with soap and water.

Roller printing is very good for making: wrapping paper, printing borders on posters, writing paper, place mats or paper cups.

PRINTING LETTERS

You Need: A sheet of thick paper; pencil; ruler; scissors.

To Make the Stencil: rule a line across the top of the sheet, then rule another line 2.5cm below it. Draw these strips down the page leaving a 2cm gap between them. Divide each strip into boxes 2cm wide. In every other box draw a letter of the alphabet, and the numbers 0-9. Cut out the letters and numbers and your stencils are ready to use.

POSTERS

CARDS

FOLDERS

WRAPPING PAPER

TABLE MATS

ENVELOPES

BOOKCOVERS

PAPERCUPS

PAPER PLATES

PICTURES

INVITATIONS

CLOTHES SEE GROOVY CLOTHES.

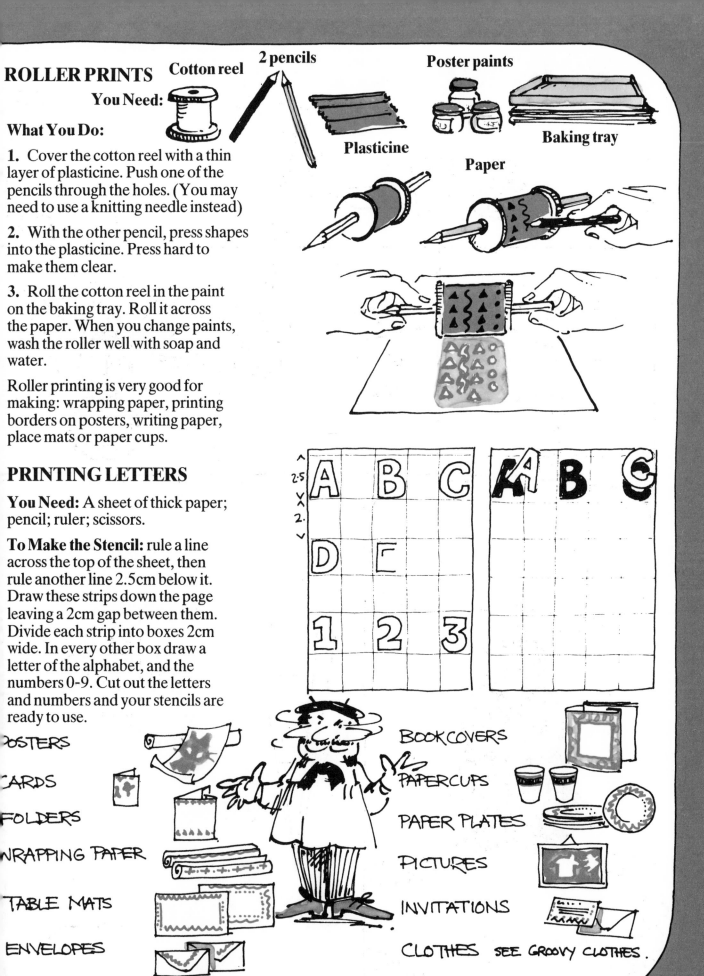

SCIENCE EXPERIMENTS

A VOLCANIC ERUPTION

You Need:

What You Do: INK   GLASS   CARD

FACT

A cubic inch of air contains 420,000,000,000,000,000,000,000 molecules.

Each molecule collides with other molecules 50,000,000,000 times a second.

① Make a small hole in the middle of the card.

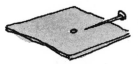

② Half fill the glass with cold water.

③ Fill up half a bottle of ink with hot water.

Place the card over the top of the glass. Quickly upturn them on to the top of the bottle.

④ A volcano of ink rises into the glass!

WHY?

The molecules in warm water are lighter, have less gravity, than those in cold water — and so the warm water rises!
This is called **CONVECTION!**

FACT

*Crystals **grow**. Their shapes gradually build up.*

WHAT ARE YOU SEEING?

Sometimes our brains are fooled by the things we see. These are called **OPTICAL ILLUSIONS** — when we see things which are not really true. What can you see below?

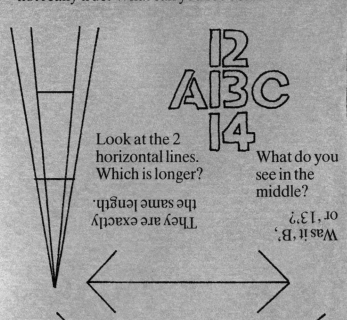

Look at the 2 horizontal lines. Which is longer?

They are exactly the same length.

What do you see in the middle?

Was it 'B', or '13'?

Which line is longer?

They are the same length

SCIENCE IN THE KITCHEN

We eat sugar and salt every day. Did you know they are both crystals?

With a magnifying glass or hand lens have a close look at them. The structure of each crystal is beautiful. You will see that crystals of the same kind are mainly the same shape.

Have a close look at some of the other things in the kitchen: mustard powder; pepper and other spices; tea leaves or even your cornflakes. Have a look at lots of things to see which ones are crystals.

You will see: Crystals have a **regular** shape. Things like tea or flour are **uneven.**

MAKE A JET BOAT

You Need: A metal soap dish or a small tin without the top; an empty round metal tin (a polish tin will do); wire or pipe cleaners; a nightlight candle; a small nail; a hammer.

What You Do:

1. With the nail and hammer make a small hole in the bottom of the round tin, near the side. You may need to ask an adult to help you.

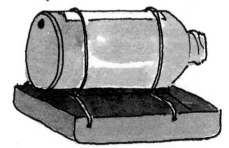

2. Mount the tin, as shown, on top of the dish or tin with the wire or pipe cleaners. The little hole must be at the top.

3. Fill the round tin half full with hot water.

4. Put the nightlight in the dish under the 'boiler'. Fill your bath with water.

5. Ask an adult to light the nightlight.

NIGHT LIGHT

WATER

Then put your jet boat at one end of the bath. As soon as the water boils, a jet of steam will escape from the hole and your boat will be propelled forwards.

WHY?

Isaac Newton's **3rd Law of Motion** states: Every action has an equal and opposite reaction. If you push your finger against a stone, then the stone pushes back with an equal force against your finger.

The jet of steam escaping backwards produces a force also acting backwards. A forward reaction follows and so your boat moves in a forward direction.

SCIENCE EXPERIMENTS

HOW CAN YOU TELL THE TIME?

Here are 2 easy clocks you can make:

1. You Need: a piece of black paper.

What You do: Make a hole in the middle of the paper. Stick it in middle of a south-facing window. When the sun shines you will see a black shadow in the room with a bright spot in the centre. Put a marker where the bright spot falls at each hour. When the sun shines you can tell the time!

If the sun isn't shining try this clock:

2. You Need: Kitchen scales with a pan to hold water; a piece of kitchen towel; another bowl.

1. Fill the pan half full with water. Drape the paper towel over the edge so the top end is well dipped into the water. The other end should hang clear so that it can drip into the second bowl put underneath.

2. The water will drip out through the paper towel at a steady rate. Write labels with hours and minutes to stick to the scale to record the passage of time as the weight of the water in the pan decreases.

3. When the pan is empty, you can fill it up again — and you will be able to check the time on your scales.

MAKE YOUR OWN WATER MICROSCOPE

Water can make things look **BIGGER**

You Need: A large plastic container (an old bucket or a large empty bleach bottle cut in half); sharp scissors; clear plastic cling film; string.

What You Do:

1. Cut a hole half-way down the side of the container, large enough for you to put your hand through.

2. Stretch the cling film over the top, not too tightly. Hold it in place by tying string round the container's rim.

3. Pour a little water on top of the cling film. It will dip down a bit.

4. Have a good look at what you are going to enlarge. Put it in your hand; put your hand through the hole — and look at the object through your microscope. Note the different things you can see.

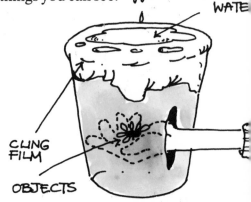

A LITTLE WATER

CLING FILM

OBJECTS

TIP: Try holding things near the water and further away. Try the film tighter or looser. See which magnifies best.

HOURS

KITCHEN TOWEL

BOWL

GROW A MINIATURE JUNGLE

You Need:

PENCIL
THREAD
BAIT
(RICE OR CORN)
JAR OF POND WATER
MAGNIFYING GLASS

What You Do:

1. Fill a jar with pond or rain water. Scoop out any solid bits.

2. Tie one end of the thread round the bait and the other round the pencil. Suspend the bait in the water.

3. Leave it for a few days.

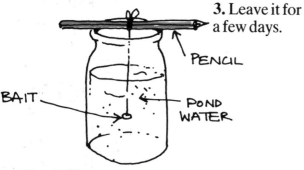

PENCIL
BAIT
POND WATER

You Will See:

1. First to develop are delicate white tubes. These are simple fungi called **hyphae.**

2. Bacteria soon form to feed on the plant food.

3. Then **Paramecium** and other **cillates** swim between the hyphae and feed on the bacteria.

4. You may then get **rotifers** which will feed on the cillates.

The more water you have in the jar the longer your jungle will last.

Look at your jungle through your magnifying glass.

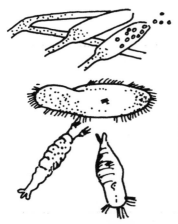

PASS A WIRE THROUGH AN ICE CUBE

You Need: an ice cube; thin wire about 15cm long; 2 pencils; a bottle.

What You Do:

1. Make handles at each end of the wire by wrapping the wire end around the middle of each pencil.

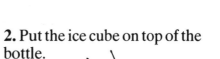

2. Put the ice cube on top of the bottle.

ICE CUBE
PRESS DOWN FIRMLY

3. Put the middle of the wire on top of the ice cube. Hold a handle in each hand. Press down firmly.

4. Gradually the wire will cut its way through the ice cube — and come out at the bottom — but the ice cube will be in one piece!

WHY?

The pressure makes the ice cube under the wire melt. As it melts, the ice steals heat from the ice surrounding it. This colder ice then re-freezes the water after the wire has passed through it.

39

IN THE WORKSHOP

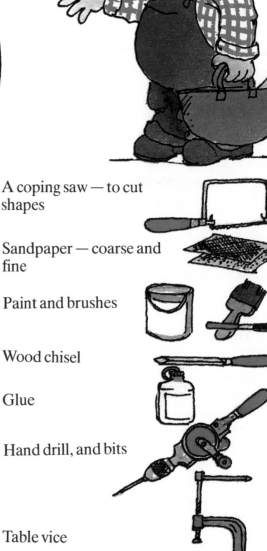

Wood has a lovely texture and beautiful graining. Things made from wood look lovely.

YOUR TOOL BOX

Keep your tools in a special box. Below are the basic tools you need. Look for them in second-hand shops, or in the 'For Sale' adverts in your local paper. Look after your tools and they will last. If they need to be sharpened, take them to an expert.

These Are The Essential Tools You Will Need:

A small saw

One or two files for wood and metal. Try and get a half-round one

An old pair of scissors

One small and one large screwdriver

A pair of pliers — to cut wire and straighten nails

Pincers for removing nails

Ruler

Box of nails of different sizes; pins; screws

Hammer

A sharp knife

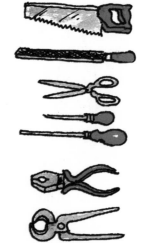

A coping saw — to cut shapes

Sandpaper — coarse and fine

Paint and brushes

Wood chisel

Glue

Hand drill, and bits

Table vice

Workbench — if possible

Before you start read the TIPS on Page 43.

SAFETY FIRST

Work carefully and think about what you are doing and you will avoid silly accidents.

Big cuts: Press the wound hard with a clean tissue or your hands. Find or call someone for help **AT ONCE.**

Small cuts: Wash in cold water; dry and put on a plaster.

Splinters: Sterilize a needle or tweezers in the blue part of a flame. Make sure you get all the splinter out. Wash it and cover with a plaster.

Bruises: Hold under cold water.

MOST OF ALL — BE CAREFUL!

YOUR JUNK BOX

All sorts of scrap can be useful for things you are making. Get a large carton — or ask your greengrocer for an empty fruit crate — to make your junk box.

These are just a few of the things to look out for and collect:

TIP: Look carefully at how things are made. Something in your junk box will probably do the job.

Old cotton reels
Scraps of wood
Scraps of metal
Wire
Nails
Springs
Corks
Rubber tubing
Jam jars
String

Hooks
Buttons
Small wooden boxes
Cardboard
Metal skewers
Wooden rods
Empty tins
Empty matchboxes
Balsa, plywood
Wheels

Here are a few simple things to make. For more difficult things, like a table, look at books specialising in simple woodwork.

STILTS — walk tall, and TALLER and TALLER!

You Need: 2 pieces of softwood 120cm x 4cm x 4cm; 1 piece of softwood 15cm x 15cm x 4cm; 4 coach bolts 11.5cm x 6mm; 4 washers to fit; 4 wing nuts to fit.
Tools: Pencil; ruler; table vice; small saw; hand drill; sharp knife; rasp; sandpaper; paintbrush; paint or varnish.

What You Do:

1. On the small piece of wood, measure 7cm along the edge. Draw a line down the middle. Hold the wood on your work-bench with the vice, as shown, and saw it down the middle for the foot rests.

2. On each long piece of wood, measure and mark 4 places for holes. Mark the first hole 13cm from the end, and then 7.5cm apart. Drill the holes right through the wood.

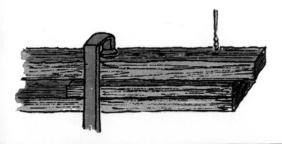

3. Place one foot rest so that it is under 2 holes on the leg, as shown. Put a pencil through the holes to mark their position on the foot rest. Drill the holes right through the foot rest. Do the same with the second ones.

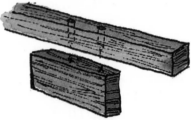

4. Sandpaper all the surfaces smooth. With the rasp round off the top edges. Paint or varnish all the wood.

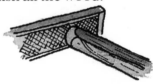

5. When they are dry, bolt the foot rests to the stilts.

Make sure the wing nuts are on the outside and are tight!

IN THE WORKSHOP

FLOWER PRESS

You Need: 2 pieces of plywood 9mm x 30cm x 30cm; 4 coach bolts 7.5cm x 6mm; 4 wing nuts and washers to fit; 7 pieces of double-faced corrugated cardboard 29cm x 29cm; 12 pieces of blotting paper 29cm x 29cm.

Tools: Coarse sandpaper; pencil; ruler; piece of waste wood; hand drill with a bit large enough to make a hole for the bolts; hammer; scissors.

What You Do:

1. Smooth the edges with sandpaper.

2. Draw diagonal lines across the wood. Measure 3cm along the line in each corner, from the edge, and mark it.

3. Put the waste wood under the boards before drilling. Then drill a hole right through each board at the place marked.

4. Push the bolts through the holes of one piece of plywood to make the base. If they are tight, gently tap them through with the hammer.

5. Check the cardboard and blotting paper are the same size. Cut off each corner so they miss the bolts.

6. Put a piece of cardboard on top of the base; then 2 pieces of blotting paper; then cardboard, and so on until all the pieces are used up.

7. Put the bolts through the top piece of plywood. Hold it in place with the nuts and washers.

8. Decorate the top with paint.

WOODEN CUT-OUTS

You can make wooden animals, trees, houses, people — or anything you want — from wood. You may not get it right first time — so be patient and try again.

You Need: Plywood; paper; paint brush; paint or varnish, or wax.
Tools: Coping saw; file; vice; glue.

What You Do:

1. Draw your shape on a piece of paper. Glue it to the plywood.

2. Hold the wood firmly in your vice.

3. With the coping saw, cut around the shape, just outside the line.

4. Once you have cut away the surrounding wood it is easier to shape the difficult bits. Then smooth the shape with the file.

When you press your flowers: Undo the washers; take off the top and lay the flowers on the blotting paper. Re-assemble and leave until they are pressed.

Pressed flowers make lovely pictures and cards.

To Make A Collection: Glue the flowers on to paper. Write the name of the flower underneath and where and when you found it.

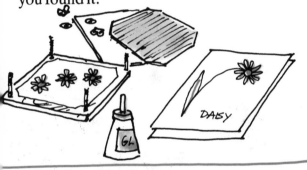

5. Paint it or polish it with wax.

TIP: If any bits break off — glue them back on.
TIP: Be careful when you saw along the grain, as the wood may split.

USEFUL TIPS

Glueing: Clean the 2 surfaces. Glue as quickly as possible. Hold the 2 surfaces tightly together.

Sandpapering: It is easier if you wrap the sandpaper around a wooden block.

Painting: Clean the surface. Stir the paint. Use a soft brush. Cover the surface evenly with a thin coat.

Boring Holes in Wood: If you don't have a drill — use a chisel for large holes; and a metal skewer for small ones.

Boring Holes in Tin: Put the tin on a piece of soft wood. Punch a hole in it using a hammer and nail.

Sawing: Make sure the blade is firmly in the handle. **NEVER CUT WOOD WITHOUT RESTING IT ON SOME-THING.** Try and hold it in a vice or clamp.

Hammering: Check the hammer head is secure. Start by gently tapping the nail. Nails should go half-way through both pieces of wood. Don't put 2 nails along the same grain or you will split the wood. Nail through a thinner piece of wood into a thicker one.

Glue: If you get glue on you or on any furniture — wipe it off at once.

Screwing: Start the hole with a drill. Put in the screw and screw firmly with your screwdriver.

Filing: Hold your file or rasp in both hands. Pull backwards and forwards across the wood. It cuts on the forward stroke.

Chiselling: Chisels cut by slicing between the fibres of the wood. Tap your chisel gently with a small block of wood to cut.

Holding the Wood: Put pieces of scrap timber between the vice and the wood to protect it.

FACT: *The largest tree on Earth is a giant Sequoia Pine in California. It's called General Sherman. It measures 31m in circumference at its base; is 83m high and weighs 2000 tonnes.*

IT'S ALL IN THE CARDS

CARD FLIP (1 or more players)

You Need: A large saucepan; a pack of cards.

How To Play: Place the pan about 3 metres from a door. Use the doorway as your flipping line. Divide the cards equally between the players.

Take it in turns to flip the cards, one by one, into the pan from the flipping line. Count how many you got in. The player with most in wins a point. 5 points wins the game.

CARD CASTLES

2 Tent Base:

Make 2 tents, as shown, with the bottoms about 2.5cm apart. Lay another card on the top to form the base of your next layer. The more tents the higher your castle can be.

FLIP SNAP (1-2 players)

Your Need: A pack of cards.

How To Play: Divide the cards equally. Player 1 drops 1, 2 or 3 cards (one at a time) from the waist so they 'flip' before hitting the ground.

Player 2 drops the same number of cards, trying to match Player 1's cards, (face up or face down).

If they match, Player 2 keeps the cards, and starts the new round. The first player to hold all the cards wins.

4 Walled Tent Base:

Make one tent. Rest a card against each end of the tent. Add 2 more walls, then a roof on either side. See if you can build a second layer!

FACTS

A card castle 51 stories high was built by a man in Texas.

Half the words meaning trickery and deceit in the English language come from playing cards.

In the 15th and 16th centuries the church outlawed all sports and games on Sundays in Europe — except for cards!

TIP: Build on the floor, but not a slippery one. Use old cards — the surface won't be so slippery.

TIP: Great patience is needed.

44

CARD GAMES

An Easy Way To Shuffle Cards:

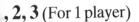

Divide the deck in half. In each hand loosely hold each half. Place one half on top of the other and gently jiggle the top half into the bottom half by moving the cards from side to side. Do this twice to shuffle.

1, 2, 3 (For 1 player)

Shuffle the cards. Then count: ace, 2,3,4,5,6,7,8,9,10,jack,queen,king, ace,2,3,4 and so on. Each time you count, turn over a card from the deck. If the card you turn over matches what you say — you lose, and have to start again.

The Aim: to get to the last card in the pack without matching a card you turn over with what you count.

AN AMAZING CARD TRICK!

You Need: A pack of cards; an accomplice; a blindfold; a victim.

The Trick: Lay 9 cards, face down, on the table. Then blindfold yourself. Ask your victim to choose one card, and to touch the chosen card. You are going to tell him which card he has chosen.

The Magic: Take off the blindfold. Your accomplice points at each card. Then you can announce which card was chosen. The **position** your accomplice touches each card, shows the position of **THE** card on the table. If every card is touched in the bottom left-hand corner, then the chosen card is the one at the bottom left-hand corner of the table.

FACT

There are 52 cards in a deck of playing cards. Add up the numbers of letters in the words that name all the cards: ace; two; three; four; five; six; seven; eight; nine; ten; jack; queen; king. they add up to 52!

The Dealer: Before you start the game, cut the pack between the players. Whoever has the highest card, deals.

OLD MAID (Any number of players)

Aim: To make pairs and discard them, and avoid ending up with the Old Maid.

How to Play: Take out the jokers. The dealer removes one queen, without saying which one, shuffles and deals all the cards.

The players look at their cards to see if they can make any pairs. If they can, they put them face up on the table.

The player on the dealer's left turns to the player on his left and holds up his cards, in a fan, with the backs to the player. The player takes a card. If she can make a pair with it, it is put on the table. If not, she keeps it and offers her cards, in a fan, to the player on her left.

Continue until all the cards are paired — and someone is left with the Old Maid. The winner has most pairs.

How Many Card Games Do You Know?

45

PUPPET PARADE

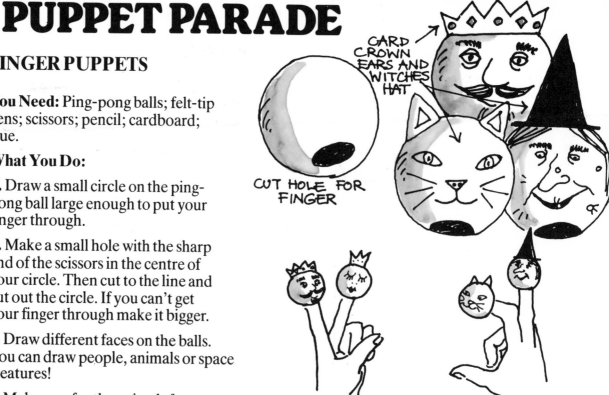

CARD CROWN EARS AND WITCHES HAT

CUT HOLE FOR FINGER

FINGER PUPPETS

You Need: Ping-pong balls; felt-tip pens; scissors; pencil; cardboard; glue.

What You Do:

1. Draw a small circle on the ping-pong ball large enough to put your finger through.

2. Make a small hole with the sharp end of the scissors in the centre of your circle. Then cut to the line and cut out the circle. If you can't get your finger through make it bigger.

3. Draw different faces on the balls. You can draw people, animals or space creatures!

4. Make ears for the animals from cardboard, and glue them on. You can also make a crown for a king, or hats.

Many museums have puppet collections. Ask your local museum where to go to see them.

HOW TO MAKE A VERY SIMPLE STAGE:

You Need: A cardboard box; wrapping paper; kitchen foil or crêpe paper; scissors; sticky tape.

What You Do: Cut the box in half lengthwise (unless it is a long narrow box when you can use it as it is). Stick the paper on the front, the top and the 2 sides. Put the box on a table with the open back facing you. You can keep your props and finger puppets in the back so you can make quick changes of character.

SILVER FOIL

KEEP PUPPETS IN HERE.

GLOVE PUPPETS

These instructions are for a girl puppet. You can alter the details to make any kind of person. Sew on ears, whiskers or a trunk for different animals.

You Need: An old sock; a piece of material twice as big as your hand and forearm; a small piece of thin cardboard (for the neck); cotton wool; wool for the hair; needle and cotton; a long piece of paper; pencil; glue; sticky labels; buttons.

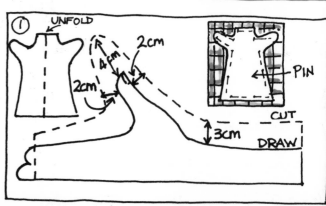

① UNFOLD

2cm

4cm

2cm

PIN

CUT

3cm

DRAW

To Make The Body:

1. Fold the paper in half. Put your hand on it, as shown, with your second finger on the fold. Draw round your hand and forearm.

2. Take your hand off. Measure 3cm away from the line of your thumb and forearm. Draw another line. Draw the line up your fingers and across the top, as shown. Cut it out; unfold it and pin it to the back of the material, which is folded in half.

3. Cut out the shape. Sew the 2 pieces together with running stitches (not the top and bottom). Turn the body inside out.

The Head:

1. Stuff the foot of the old sock with cotton wool. Make a card tube which is thinner at the top. Glue its edges together.

2. Put the tube, for the neck, in the sock. Tie it in place with wool. Cut the sock off at the bottom of the tube.

Joining Up:

Dab glue inside the top of the body, and at the bottom of the neck. Glue them together. Hide the join with a strip of material to act as a scarf.

The Hair:

Cut the wool in pieces of the same length. Glue them to the top of the head so they all hang downwards. Shorter pieces can be glued forwards to make a fringe.

Or — glue on cotton wool; fur fabric or scrunched up tissue paper for hair and beards.

Face: Noses, mouths and eyes can be made from sticky labels; sewing on beads or sticking on felt. Funny noses can be made from sponge and stuck on.

Headresses: Hats; crowns; magician's hat can be made out of cardboard.

Try writing a simple play — or make a play out of a story you know.

FINISHED PUPPET.

TIP: YOU have to give your puppet life. Think what its character is; practise movements; use its arms to show emotions like surprise.

TIP: Go to puppet shows and watch! Keep scenery simple.

How many things can you get your puppet to do?

HOLDING YOUR PUPPET

Your thumb goes in one arm; your 2 middle fingers go in the middle; your 2 end fingers go in the other arm.

TIP: Your wrist is your puppet's waist.

TIP: To turn the head: press the 2 neck fingers against the edge of the tube and move your fingers round.

Props: Use and make your props. For example:
A broom: tie small twigs to a large one.
Flower pots: from yoghurt pots.
Magician's wand: from a pencil.
Trees: from cardboard.

47

STRING IT UP

COLLECTING STRING

There are many different kinds of string, including jute, nylon, and raffia. Collect as many as you can and compare them.

Here are some ways you can twist, knot, plait, coil and fray string to give you different patterns and textures:

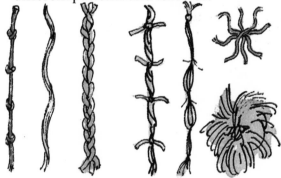

STRING PICTURES

You can make very interesting and unusual pictures with string, particularly if you use different kinds of string and use the different patterns and textures shown above.

You Need: Different kinds of string; thin card or material; glue; scissors; paper and pencil.

What You Do:

1. Make a rough drawing on a piece of paper to decide how you are going to use your string—which bits will look nice plaited or knotted; which frayed or coiled.

2. Stick the string on to thin card or material. Use material in your picture.

A KNOT HOLDER

You Need: 4 pieces of string, 1 metre long.

What You Do:

1. Make 2 pairs with the string, and lay them across each other, as shown.

2. Pick up the 4 strings where they cross, and tie a knot just below this point.

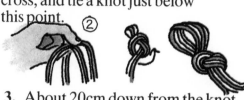

3. About 20cm down from the knot, tie each pair of strings in a knot, as shown. (It's a strong knot.)

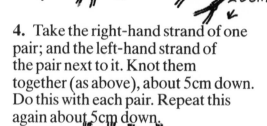

4. Take the right-hand strand of one pair; and the left-hand strand of the pair next to it. Knot them together (as above), about 5cm down. Do this with each pair. Repeat this again about 5cm down.

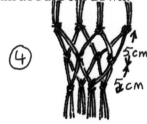

5. Then about 7.5cm down tie all the strands together in one large knot —and your holder is complete.

To Make A String Bag: Just start knotting about 10cm down from the main knot and then every 2.5cm down.

PLANT HOLDER

STRING BAG

STRING PATTERNS

Another way of making pictures with string is to wind the string around pins to make intricate patterns. Here is a **Butterfly Pattern** to make:

You Need: A piece of polystyrene foam; pins; thin string or thread (different colours look nice); pencil; ruler.

What You Do:

1. Draw 2 lines; 20cm long, as shown. Put a pin at the top of each line, then put in pins, 2cm apart, all the way down each line.

2. At the **top** of the left line, mark the pin '1', and then number **down.** The **bottom** of the right line mark '1', and then number **up.**

3. Tie your thread around **Top 1.** Take it across and wind it around **Bottom 1.** Then around **Bottom 2,** and up and across to **Top 2.** Then wind it around **Top 3** and down and across to **Bottom 3.**

4. Do this through all the numbers and your pattern will build up. When you get to the last number, tie the string in a knot around the last pin and your butterfly pattern is complete.

You can paint the foam—or cover it with foil before you begin.

Experiment with other shapes. Draw round a plate to get a circle; or draw 2 lines wider apart than for the butterfly; or of different lengths. Several patterns on the same board makes an unusual picture.

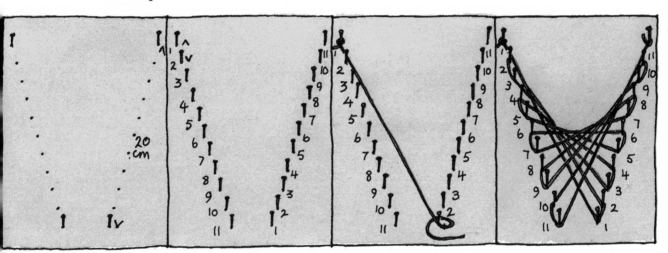

THIS KNOT CAN UNTIE ITSELF!

You Need: A piece of string or rope.

The Trick: Hold one end of the string in each hand. Twist the ends around each other once, then hold them in the same hands again.

Tie one knot above the twist; pull on the ends and sides of the string at once, and tighten the knot.

The Magic: The knot will stay knotted —but if you take hold of one end of the string and shake it hard—the knot will dissolve!

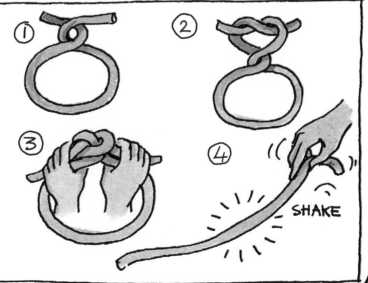

STRING IT UP!

CAT'S CRADLE (For 2 players)

This is an old medieval game where a loop of string is passed from one player to the other by making a series of patterns.

You Need: A piece of string about 1 metre long. Knot the ends together.

To start the game:

Player 1: Loop the string around both hands. Then take the near string with your right fingers and pass it across your left palm. Loop it around the back of your left hand, as shown.

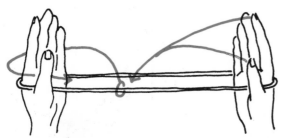

Do this with your right hand, ending like this:

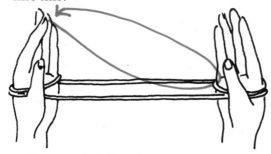

Slip your left forefinger under the right palm string. Pull the string tight. Do the same with your right forefinger, so you look like this:

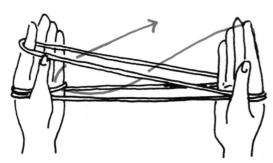

This pattern is called **'cat's cradle'**.

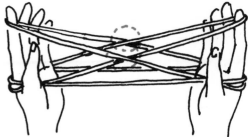

Player 2: Pull the strings apart with your finger and thumb. Take crossed strings under the parallel strings and up into the middle. Widen your forefingers and thumbs to take the tension, and lift the string from Player 1.

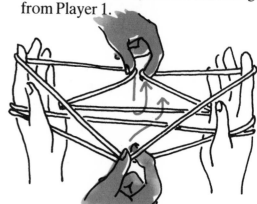

This pattern is called **'bed'**.

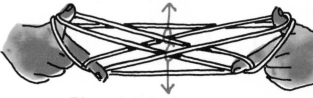

Player 1: Take the crossed strings. Pull them apart. Take them under the parallel strings and up into the middle. Widen your forefingers and thumbs to take the tension and Player 2 can slip out of the string.

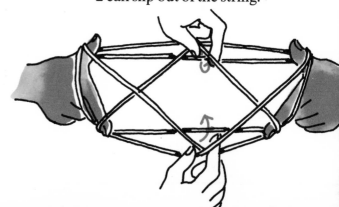

This pattern is called **'2 candles.'**

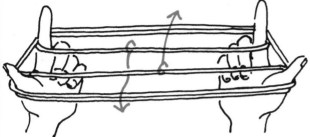

Player 2: Hook the little finger of each hand under the inside string of the opposite side. Pull the strings over. Don't let go while you push your forefingers and thumbs under the parallel strings and up into the centre.

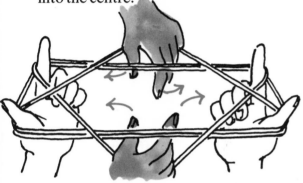

Player 1 can slip out. This pattern is called **'manger'.**

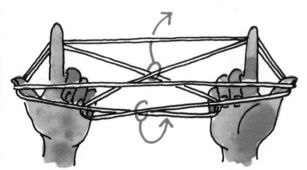

Player 1: Take the crossed strings. Pull them outwards, up and over the parallel strings and down into the centre. Open your forefingers and thumbs wide to hold the string. Player 2 can slip out now. This is called **'St. Andrew's Cross'.**

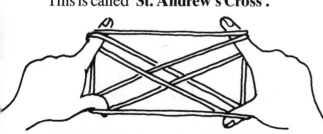

How many more moves and patterns can you create? How many stages can you go before you drop the string or fail to hold a pattern!

PLAITING

You Need: 3 strands of string (try and use different colours).

What You Do:

1. Take the right-hand string. Pass it over the centre one and under the left-hand string.

2. Then carry the new left-hand string over the centre and under the right-hand strand.

3. Carry on and you will make flat braid that can be used for bracelets, belts or headbands.

To make a wider braid, use 5 strands.

CHAIN BRAID

You Need: A strand of string; pencil.

What You Do:

Tie one end around a pencil—then follow the instructions in the drawings to make the braid.
Use it for a belt; a shoulder strap or as a bracelet.

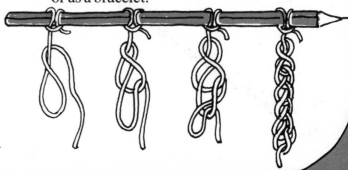

HOCUS POCUS MAGIC!

10 TIPS

1. **PRACTISE** each trick.
2. Plan for **DISASTERS**. If everything goes wrong, pretend it was planned, and tell a joke.
3. **REHEARSE** what you are going to say.
4. **PLAN** your show. **DON'T** do similar tricks near each other. **DON'T** make the show too long.
5. Don't keep trying a trick that **FAILS.**
6. **INCLUDE** some tricks for the person in the audience who thinks they know it all!
7. **DON'T** be too adventurous.
8. **NEVER** tell your secrets.
9. Make sure your show is **FUN.**
10. **DON'T** get stage fright and panic.

Difficulty Symbols
: a simple trick

: a more difficult trick

: this trick needs practice!

MAKE YOUR OWN MAGIC WAND

1. Find a round stick about 1.2cm thick, and 30cm long.

2. Sandpaper it smooth, then paint it with a black enamel glossy paint. Let it dry.

2. Wrap sellotape or masking tape about 2.5cm from each end.

4. Paint both ends with white enamel paint. Remove the tape when it's dry.

THE MYSTERIOUS GLASS

You Need: a sheet of paper; a glass; a victim.

The Trick: Put the glass on top of the paper. Ask if anyone can remove the paper from under the glass without touching the glass. If your victim wants to try and whip away the paper, stop them by saying you don't want a broken glass.

The Magic: Roll up the paper from the end, very tightly. Don't touch the glass! The middle of the rolled paper pushes the glass away!

ALL IN A KNOT

You Need: 3 scarves and a victim.

The Trick: Two of the scarves are tied together. Show your victim all 3 scarves. What your victim has to do is put the third scarf between the two others without tearing them, and without untying the knot!

The Magic: The third scarf is tied to the end of the other two! Amazing!

THE MOVING COIN

You Need:

PLATE GLASS 2 COINS ENVELOPE SOAP

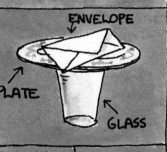

The Trick:

Place one coin in the envelope.

Put the plate on top of the glass. Then put the envelope on top of the plate.

Tap it with your magic wand, and the coin goes into the glass, through the plate.

Practise to see how much soap you need.

The Magic:

COIN

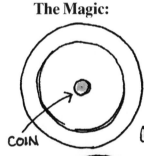

You had already stuck the 2nd coin under the plate with a bit of damp soap. The sharp tap of your wand dislodges the coin.

The first coin was never in the envelope. You dropped it into your lap, or the pocket of your magic table.

COIN DROPS

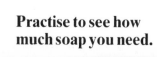

53

HOCUS POCUS MAGIC!

THE FLYING THIMBLE

You Need: A thimble; a victim.

The Trick: Put the thimble on your second finger. Tell your victim you are going to throw it to them. But where is it? Is it behind their ear?

The Magic: You **pretend** to throw the thimble. Really you have bent your finger back and tucked the thimble between your palm and your thumb. No-one will see. They will be watching the space between you and your victim. To produce it from behind their ear, bend your finger back and put it on.

LOOPY LOOPS

You Need: 4 long strips of newspaper; glue; scissors; a victim.

The Trick: Glue 2 strips of paper into 2 loops. Ask your victim to cut one of the loops through the centre. You do the same with your loop. Your victim has 2 separate loops. Yours is one large one! Glue the other 2 strips into 2 loops. Ask your victim to cut his loop through the centre again. He has 2 loops! You have 2 loops joined together.

The Magic: Before you stick **your** first loop together, put one **twist** in the strip.

Put **2 twists** in your second strip before gluing it.

MAKES TWO LOOPS

1 TWIST →

MAKES ONE BIG LOOP

2 TWISTS

MAKES INTERLOCKING LOOPS

MATCHBOX MAGIC

The Trick: Hold up the matchbox. Shake it. It's empty! Open it upside-down. No matches fall out! Tap it with your wand — the matches fall into your hand!

The Magic: Cut one match to fit the width of the box. Push it sideways across the box to hold the other matches in place. When you tap the box, it will fall out. The matches will appear!

You Need: a full matchbox

Practise this trick.

THE MIGHTY MIND

You Need: a piece of paper; 9 pencils; a hat; a blindfold.

The Trick: Tear the paper into 9 pieces. Give 9 members of the audience a piece of paper and a pencil. As you give the paper and pencil to them, ask them their name and ask them to write it on the paper. Collect all 9 pieces of paper. Put them in the hat. Blindfold yourself, then pick from the hat one piece of paper and tell your audience the name written on it?

The Magic: Tear the sheet of paper like the rabbit. Only **one** piece of paper has 4 jagged edges. Remember who wrote on it. When you are blindfolded, you will be able to feel which piece of paper does not have a straight edge. It's magic!

MEMORIZE THIS ONE

ABRACADABRA

Magicians use magic words to make their magic work and **ABRACADABRA** *is one of them.* **ABRACADABRA** *mainly uses the first four letters of the alphabet, and when it is written in the form of a triangle, dropping one letter on each line, it is a powerful* **amulet** *(an amulet wards off all kinds of evil and danger).*

```
A B R A C A D A B R A
A B R A C A D B R
A B R A C A D B
A B R A C A D
A B R A C A
A B R A C
A B R A
A B R
A B
A
```

Why do witches and wizards always drink tea?

Because sorcerers need cuppas!

Newcomer: Bertie always wanted to be a stage magician and saw people in half.
Neighbour: *Is he an only one.*
Newcomer: Oh no. He has several half-brothers and sisters.

Overheard at Magician's Convention:
'Hi there, Terry, how's tricks?

NATURE FUN

FUN WITH LEAVES

LEAF PRINTS AND PICTURES

You Need: Different-shaped leaves; poster paints; a plate; sheets of paper; thin card; paint brush.

What You Do:

1. Spread some paint on the plate. Lay the leaf on the paint and press it gently to cover it with paint.

2. Put the leaf, paint-side down, on a sheet of paper. Put another sheet of paper on top and rub gently. Carefully remove the leaf from the paper.

3. Use different-shaped leaves in your picture. Paint the leaves, with the brush, in different colours. Try using coloured paper.

4. Your leaf prints can become the wings of a butterfly or the petals of a flower. Print them on thin card to make birthday or Christmas cards.

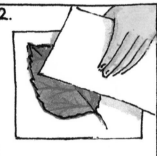
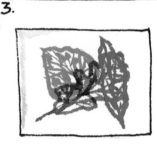

LEAF SKELETONS

You Need: Old, tough leaves; washing soda; domestic bleach; blotting paper; paint brush; paper; and old saucepan.

What You Do:
1. Half fill the pan with water. Add a tablespoon of washing soda. Put in the leaves. Simmer on the stove for an hour. **Ask a grown-up to turn on the stove.**

2. Let the water cool. Lift out the leaves. Brush away the leaf tissue with a paint brush.

3. Add ¾ cup of bleach to a bowl of water. Soak the skeletons overnight. Lift them out. Dry between 2 sheets of blotting paper.

FACT
The leaves of the Yucca plant are so stiff and sharp that Spanish colonists, in Florida, used them to protect their camps from attack.

4. Glue them to card or put them in a picture.

HE ZOO IN YOUR HOME . . .

Where To Look:

1. Behind pictures: spiders and hibernating insects.

2. Lights: attract insects.

3. Ceiling; wall corners; light fittings: house spider.

4. Behind radiators: insects.

5. Skirting boards: ants use them as a run; insects.

6. The best chair: your dog or cat.

7. Fire: an insect called a firebrat.

8. Plants: insects; mainly green and white fly.

9. Floorboards: mice; cockroaches.

10. Cellar: usually damp — look for toads, spiders and woodlice.

11. Doorstep and paths: birds, slugs and hedgehogs.

12. Kitchen: woodlice.

13. Kitchen larder and cupboards: flies; mice; beetle larvae; moths and mites.

14. Bathroom: spiders.

15. Window and window sills: birds; insects; butterfly chrysalid on the frame.

16. Chimney and T.V. aerial: birds.

17. Roof: birds.

18. Wardrobe and drawers: spiders and clothes moths.

19. Brickwork: single bees may make their home in small holes.

20. Garden shed and garage: hibernating animals like hedgehogs; chrysalids. **DO NOT DISTURB THEM.** Garden spiders.

21. Eaves and hedges: birds' nests. **DO NOT DISTURB THEM.**

Wherever you live you will find that many animals share your home with you. How many can you spot? Make a plan of your zoo.

DO NOT DISTURB THEM: (unless you have to.) Make a note of changes in your zoo.

FACTS

Flies take off into flight with a backward jump.

Moths do not eat clothes. It is their larvae who do the damage.

NATURE FUN

You Will Need: 3 medium-sized potatoes; 1 smaller one (potatoes are moist); mustard and cress seeds (seeds have food); cocktail sticks.

What You Do:

1. Make little holes with a cocktail stick in the top of the potatoes.

2. Push the seeds into the holes. The water in the potatoes will make them sprout in a couple of days.

3. Join the potatoes together with cocktail sticks, and use the sticks to make legs.

GROW A MONSTER

Gardens do not have to be flat. As long as you have water and food you can grow . . . a monster

POTATOES

COCKTAIL STICKS

SEEDS

4. The seedlings become your monster's hair. Draw a face on it with a pen.

MAGNIFYING MAGIC

You can discover the most amazing facts about plants and animals by looking at them under a hand lens or magnifying glass.

Here are some you will find easily: ants; greenfly; dandelion flowers; caterpillars; plant roots.

FACTS

*The tulip originally came from Turkey. Its name is taken from the Turkish word **Tulband**, which means 'turban'.*

Wheat is the largest single crop grown on Earth, followed by rice, maize, barley and potatoes.

GROW A GARDEN IN A SAUCER

Cut the crowns (tops) off vegetables like carrots, beetroot and parsnips (the vegetables need to be unscraped).

Stand them cut-side down in a saucer of shallow water. Place them near the light and leaves will soon start to sprout from the top.

Use different vegetables and put pretty stones around them.

BEETROOT LEAVES

CARROT LEAVES

MAKE A HERB PILLOW

You Need: Herbs and petals; a small tray; a piece of cotton material about 15cm x 20cm; a slightly larger pretty piece of material; needle and thread.

What You Do:

1. Try and collect: scented rose petals; lavender heads when the flowers have finished; mint; sweet briar; rosemary; and verbena. You need enough to cover the tray.

2. Keep the tray in your airing cupboard. Dry the flowers and leaves as you collect them. Take them out as they dry. It will take 3-4 days.

3. Make a bag from the piece of cotton, leaving one end open so you can stuff it with the herbs and flowers. When it is full, sew up the edge.

4. Make another bag with the other piece of material. Leave one end open and slip in the herb pillow.

LAVENDER

ROSE

HERB PILLOW.

MAKING MUSIC

SONG GAMES

SING-A-LONG (2 or more players)

One person sings a few lines of a song, and whoever guesses the name of the song first, wins a point. You can hum or whistle the tune. You can also limit the song to a pop song, and, for an extra point, you must name the singer.

SONGS, SONGS, SONGS
(2 or more players)

How many songs do you know? Pick a subject, for example, food; girls' names; towns. Each player must sing part of a song that mentions a town, or whichever subject you have chosen. If a player can't think of a song, they drop out until one player is left. The winner chooses the next subject.

DESERT ISLAND DISCS
Which 10 records would you take with you if you were shipwrecked on a desert island?

'Doctor, I was playing my flute, and I swallowed it!'
'Never mind. Look on the bright side. It could have been a grand piano!'

The trumpet player had been blasting away all day. There was a knock on his door. 'I live next door, Do you know I work nights?' 'No,' said the trumpet player, 'hum a few bars and I will get the melody.'

On the next few pages there are lots of ideas to show you how to make your own musical instruments. When you have made them, try playing songs or tunes you know. It is also fun to play along to records or the radio. You can do this when there is a group of you playing — or when you are on your own.

WHAT IS SOUND?

Air is made up of molecules. Even the smallest movement jostles these molecules, and cause a **disturbance.** This disturbance reaches your ears and vibrates on your eardrums. These vibrations are what you hear as sound.

SOUNDS ABOUT RIGHT

How many sounds can you hear?

Make a list of them — and you will be amazed how many different sounds there are even when you think that it is quiet.

Do you know how loud different sounds are? Here is a list of sounds. Which is the loudest?

> Normal breathing
> Food blender
> Aeroplane engine
> Busy traffic
> Whispering
> A car horn

Normal breathing
Whispering
Busy traffic
Car horn
Food blender
Aeroplane engine

60

RHYTHM BAND FOR ONE

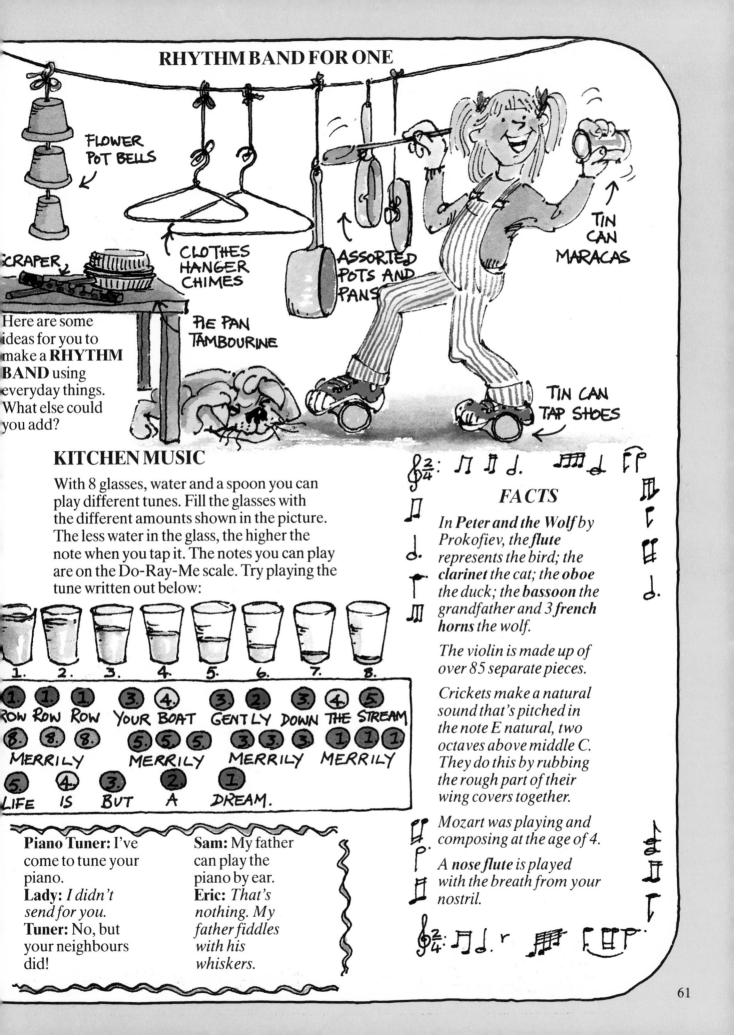

FLOWER POT BELLS

SCRAPER

CLOTHES HANGER CHIMES

PIE PAN TAMBOURINE

ASSORTED POTS AND PANS

TIN CAN MARACAS

TIN CAN TAP SHOES

Here are some ideas for you to make a **RHYTHM BAND** using everyday things. What else could you add?

KITCHEN MUSIC

With 8 glasses, water and a spoon you can play different tunes. Fill the glasses with the different amounts shown in the picture. The less water in the glass, the higher the note when you tap it. The notes you can play are on the Do-Ray-Me scale. Try playing the tune written out below:

1. 2. 3. 4. 5. 6. 7. 8.

① ① ① ③ ④ ③ ② ③ ④ ⑤
ROW ROW ROW YOUR BOAT GENTLY DOWN THE STREAM
⑧ ⑧ ⑧ ⑤ ⑤ ⑤ ③ ③ ③ ① ① ①
MERRILY MERRILY MERRILY MERRILY
⑤ ④ ③ ② ①
LIFE IS BUT A DREAM.

Piano Tuner: I've come to tune your piano.
Lady: *I didn't send for you.*
Tuner: No, but your neighbours did!

Sam: My father can play the piano by ear.
Eric: *That's nothing. My father fiddles with his whiskers.*

FACTS

*In **Peter and the Wolf** by Prokofiev, the **flute** represents the bird; the **clarinet** the cat; the **oboe** the duck; the **bassoon** the grandfather and 3 **french horns** the wolf.*

The violin is made up of over 85 separate pieces.

Crickets make a natural sound that's pitched in the note E natural, two octaves above middle C. They do this by rubbing the rough part of their wing covers together.

Mozart was playing and composing at the age of 4.

*A **nose flute** is played with the breath from your nostril.*

MAKING MUSIC

If you like music why don't you try making some of these musical instruments. All you need is a melody instrument, like a comb and paper, to play the tune, and some rhythm instruments, like the shaker or drum. Play them on your own or form a band with your friends.

COMB AND PAPER

Fold a piece of tissue paper over a clean comb. Put it between your lips and blow.

SCRAPER

File notches in a piece of wood about 30cm long. Scrape another small piece of wood across the notches to make a sound. Paint patterns on it.

SHAKER

Cut a plastic bottle in half (washing-up liquid bottles are good). Wash it out and dry it. Half fill it with rice or dried peas. Tape it together. Decorate the bottle with coloured tape.

CASTANETS

Cut 2 pieces of cardboard 3.5cm wide and 15cm long. Fold each piece in half. Punch a hole through each end, above each other. Punch holes through the centres of 4 bottle tops (ask an adult to help). Tie one top to each end of board by pushing thread through the holes. Hold your castanets between your thumb and fingers. Snap the ends to play.

CYMBALS

All you need is 2 saucepan lids to bang together.

HOSE-PIPE PIPE

Cut a short piece of hose off the hose-pipe (ask first!). Punch some holes down one side. This makes a good pipe and you can play a range of notes.

FLOWER POT BELLS

You need 3 or 4 clay flower pots, each a different size. Knot a length of rope through the hole in each pot. Push the other end through the crack in a wooden crate and knot it so the pots are hanging. Bang the pots with a stick.

DRUMS

Most hollow things can be used to make drums: half a coconut; pieces of plastic drain-pipe; a wooden cheese box; or a biscuit tin. Stretch a piece of plastic or a piece of damp cloth over the top and tie it as shown. Use your fingers or a pencil to beat it.

COCONUT DRUM

TIN DRUMS

FLOUR

BISCUITS

BOX GUITAR

Cut a small semi-circle in the side, and near one end of an empty cereal packet. Seal up the open end with tape. Use the piece of cut-out board as a bridge and stretch large rubber bands over the box and bridge, as shown. Pluck the rubber bands.

TRIANGLE

Tie some string round a fork or a wire hanger and hang it up, (you can use your arm!). Hit it with another fork.

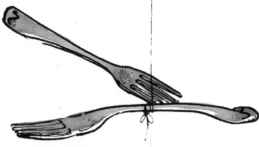

CUP BANJO

Stretch an elastic band over the mouth and bottom of a paper or plastic cup. Pluck the band where it stretches across the mouth of the cup. To increase the range of sound you can play put your finger or a pencil under the elastic on the side of the cup. When you pull it away from the side, the notes will change their sound.

JUG

Any old bottle makes a good jug. Put the top of the bottle against your lower lip. Blow across the opening. If you hold the bottle at the right angle, you will make music! Water in the bottle gives a higher note. This makes good background music for the banjo and wind instruments.

JOKES, JOKES, JOKES

Where on Earth would you find a pink elephant?

Just where you left it!

Why can't you put out a fire on the Moon?

Because you're not there!

Husband: (to wife); How did you get the car into the dining-room?
Wife: *Oh, that was easy! Through the kitchen and first turning on the right.*

A TERRIBLE TONGUE TWISTER

If the rustlers wrestled the wrestlers,
While the wrestlers rustled the rustlers,
Could the rustlers rustle the wrestlers,
While the wrestlers wrestle the rustlers?

Woman: I'll have 3 nice pork chops — and make them lean.
Butcher: *Certainly madam. Which way?*

What is the best thing to put in pies?

Your teeth.

Mechanic: Madam, the trouble with your car is that the battery's flat.
Woman: *Oh dear! What shape should it be?*

How do you make your hair dance?

With a head band!

Professor: (in a noisy class): Order!
Voice: (from the rear): *Beer!*

After the dance the young man asked the young lady if he could see her home — so she showed him a photograph of it.

What kind of coat has no pockets or buttons?

A coat of paint!

What is as big as a dinosaur and doesn't weigh an ounce?

A dinosaur's shadow.

Sue: Why is your dog wearing black wellington boots?
Jamie: *His brown ones are at the menders.*